The Great Barrier Reef

Wildlife in Pictures and AI Dreaming

JOHN PATERSON

Contents

The Great Barrier Reef

The complexity of coral reef ecosystems is not surprising given the great length of time that these ecosystems have been in existence. While the shallow water distribution of coral reefs has varied with the alternation of glacial and interglacial periods, in their broad biological form, coral reefs have existed since the Precambrian and reefs similar to present reefs have existed for around 50 million years.

Heron Reef lies in the Capricorn Group which is towards the southern end of the Great Barrier Reef. It is a lagoonal platform reef with a vegetated cay at its western end. The cay supports a tourist resort and research station. Heron Reef has been zoned as Marine Park A within the Capricornia Section of the Great Barrier Reef Marine Park, and prior to this was protected, from over-collection, by a regulation of Queensland State Fisheries. The western end of the reef is easily accessible from the cay but access to the eastern end requires the use of a small boat.

At the western end of Heron Reef, the reef flat is the sub-tidal habitat nearest to the cay. It is chiefly comprised of dead and living coral clumps which vary in size from a few centimetres in diameter to dead coral boulders or living micro-atolls with diameters of several meters. The dead coral clumps can, at certain times of the year, be obscured by a prolific growth of algae. The chief physical parameter that separates the reef flat from the lagoon is the water depth at low water spring tides. The water depth can vary from less than half a meter at the western end of the reef where sedimentation is great to more than a meter at its transition into lagoon east of the cay. The lagoon is up to six meters in depth at Heron Reef and has scattered coral outcrops which may reach the surface. At the innermost part of the reef flat (adjacent to the cay) a series of strata composed of cemented sand and coral fragments occurs. The strata are called beach rock.

The reef crest is the outer region of intertidal coral growth and is shallower than the previous zone. It is the most turbulent of all coral-reef zones being exposed to direct wave action at all stages of the tide. It has little fine sediment other than that which is trapped within the algal turf and which has accumulated under boulders. Living coral growth is usually low in profile and the general substrate is comprised of cemented reef rock strewn with broken coralline material. This material ranges in size from single coral fragments which are a few centimetres in diameter, to large boulders that are greater than two meters in diameter.

The reef slope is subtidal and supports extensive coral growth to a depth of approximately 20 meters. The coral growth tapers off to almost negligible coral cover at a depth of approximately 30 meters where the slope merges with the off-reef floor. This transition may be sudden on some reefs which possess almost vertical reef slopes, but at Heron Reef the transition is gradual. This zone is less physically controlled than are the previous zones. After periods of severe swell there may be areas of broken coral colonies but generally, as depth increases, the direct effect of wave action decreases. The substrate is of poorly sorted sediments as well as living and dead coral colonies, together with their epibiota.

The off-reef floor between Heron Reef and the adjacent reefs is over 40 meters deep and in places supports a well-developed fauna of alcyonarians and solitary hard corals along with their associated epibiota. The off-reef floor is the deepest of the reef zones and provides habitats that are clearly different from the shallow water habitats provided by the other three zones. The sediment found on the off-reef floor is varied and its composition is dependent on currents as well as on surge effects during heavy wave action.

Green Island and Upolu Cay are mid-shelf reefs in the Cairns Section of the Great Barrier Reef Marine Park. Green Island is heavily vegetated and has a resort and hotel. Upolu Cay is just north of Green Island and has grassy vegetation with many nesting seabirds.

Heron Island

Wistari Reef from the air. Heron Reef in background. (1980)

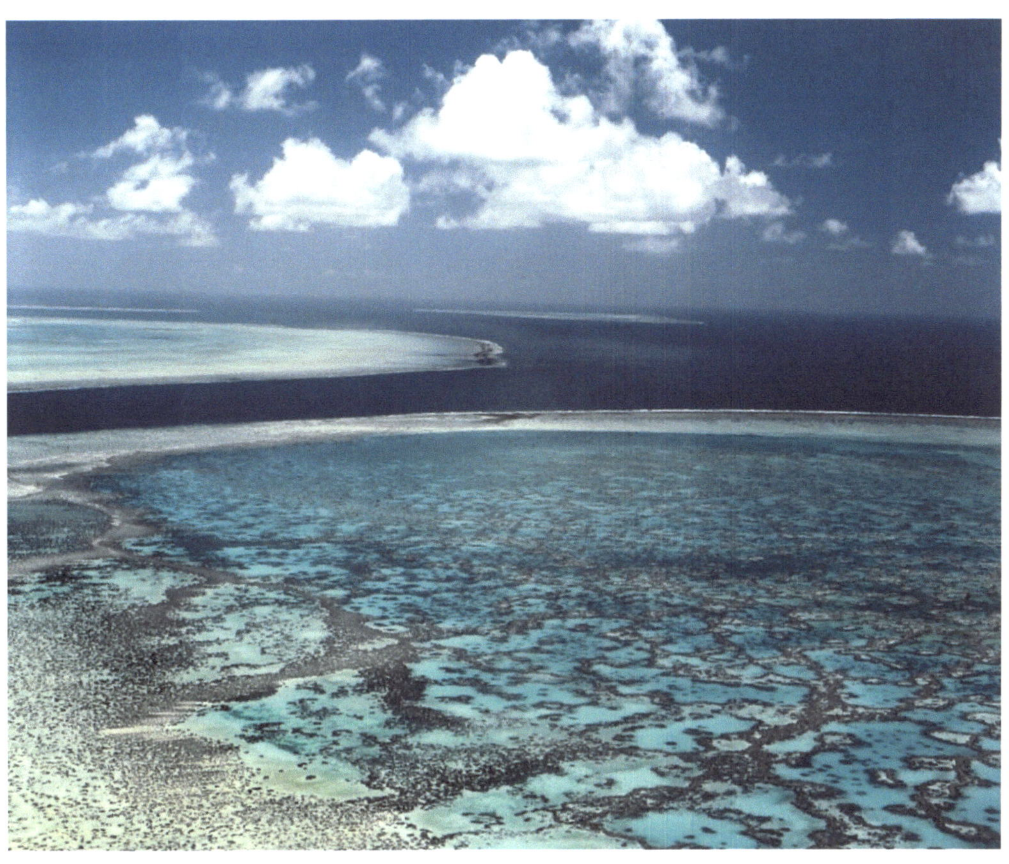

Heron Island from the air. Wistari Reef in background. (1980)

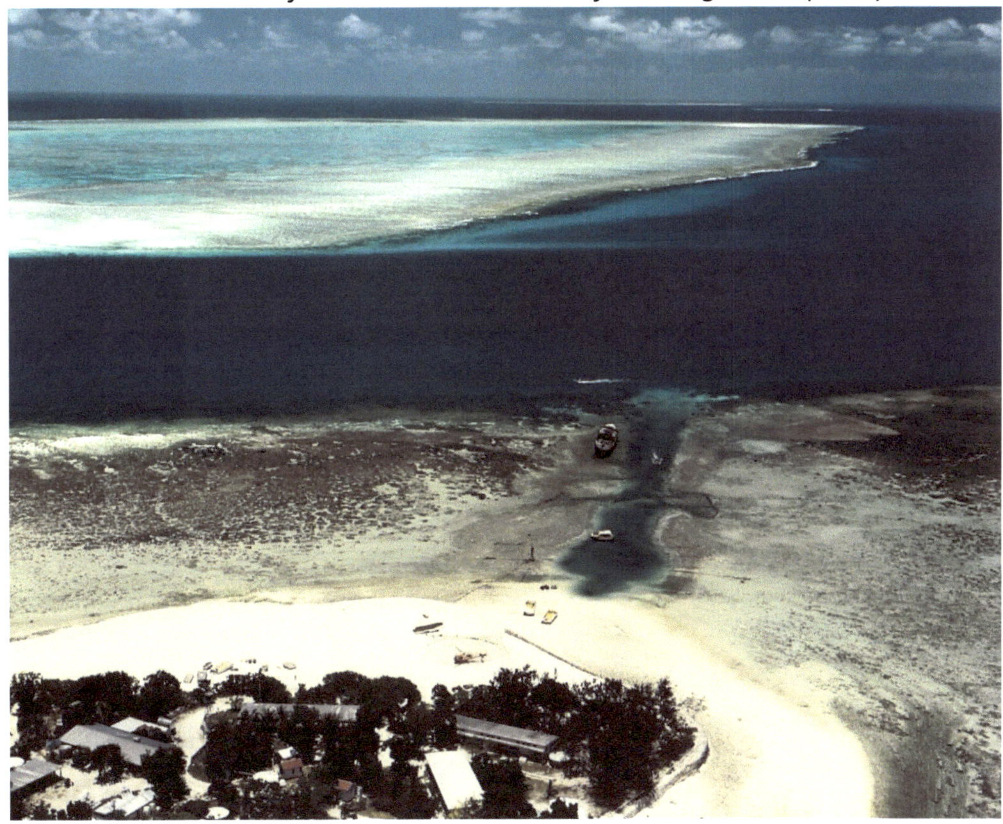

Eastern end of Heron Island. Beachrock in foreground. (1980)

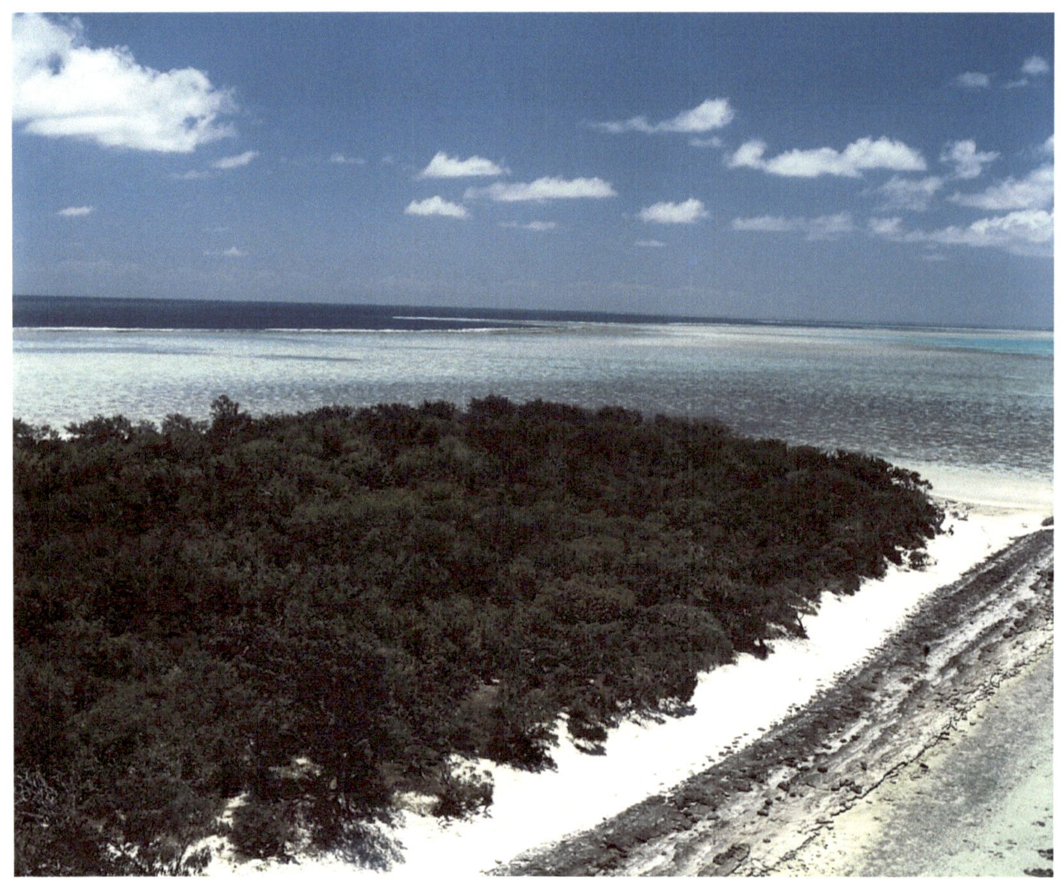

Beach rock at low tide (1980)

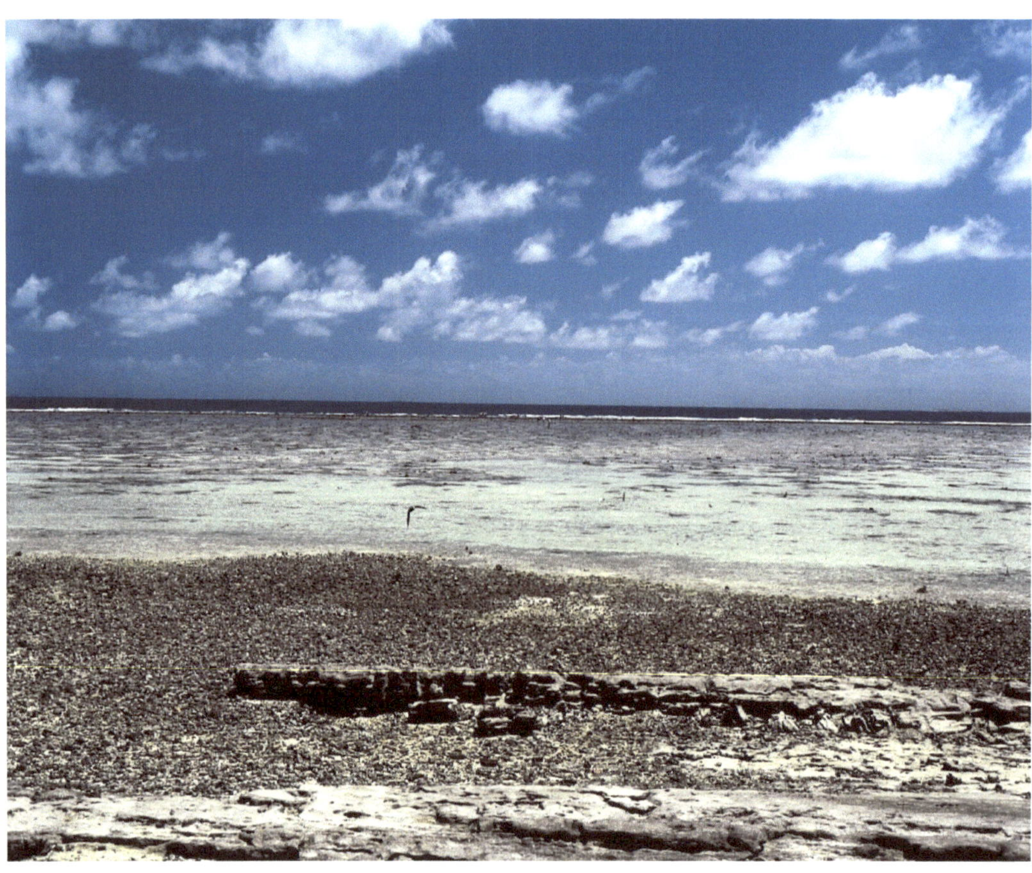

Algae and Sponges

Caulerpa racemosa

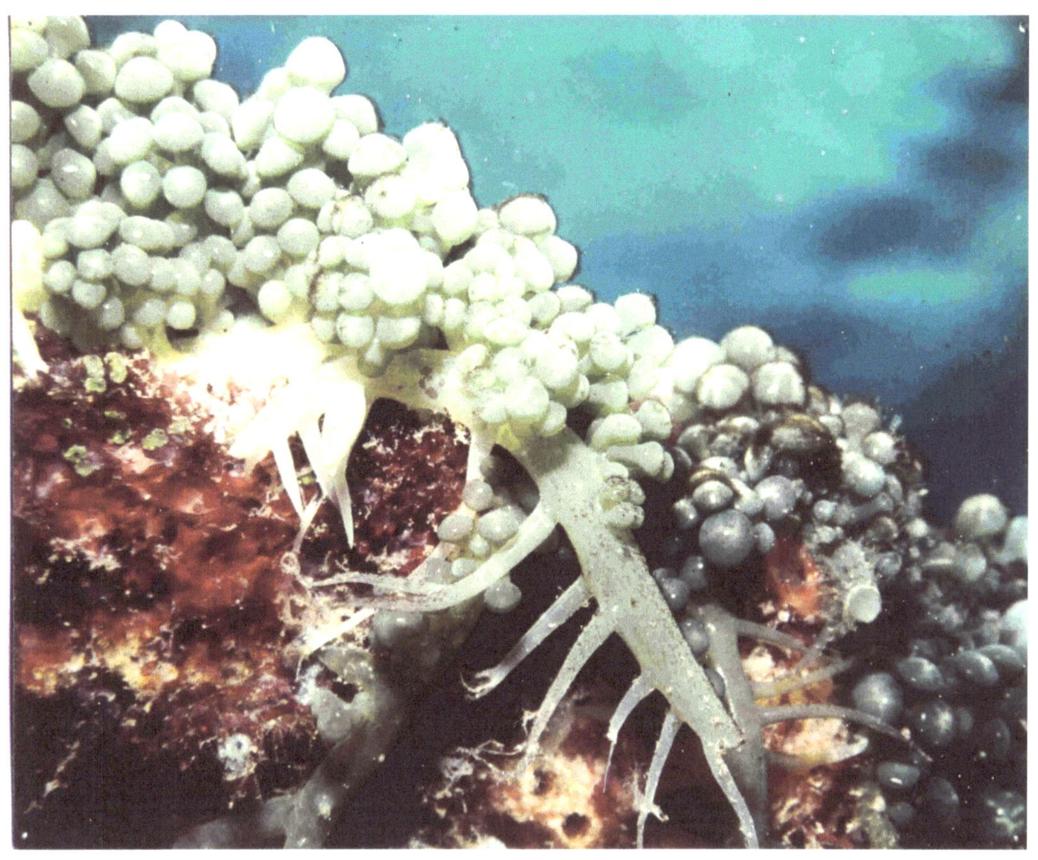

Sponge with polychaete tubes

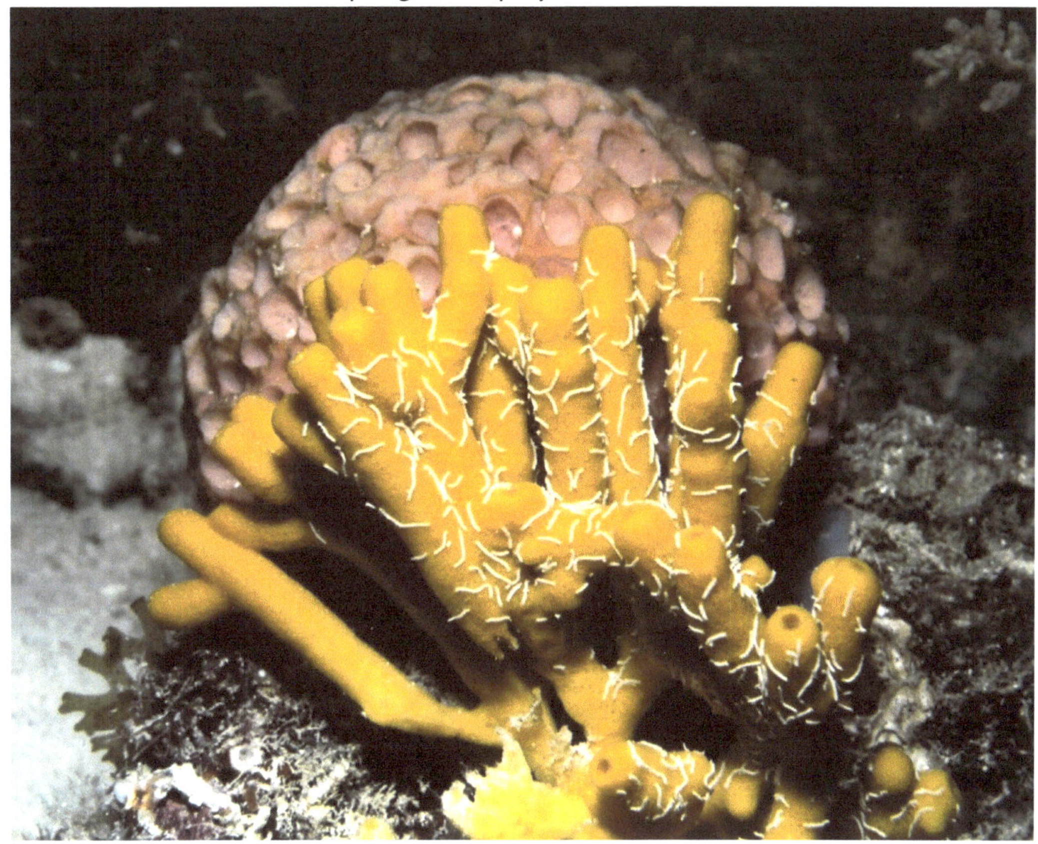

Soft Corals

Dendronepthia sp.

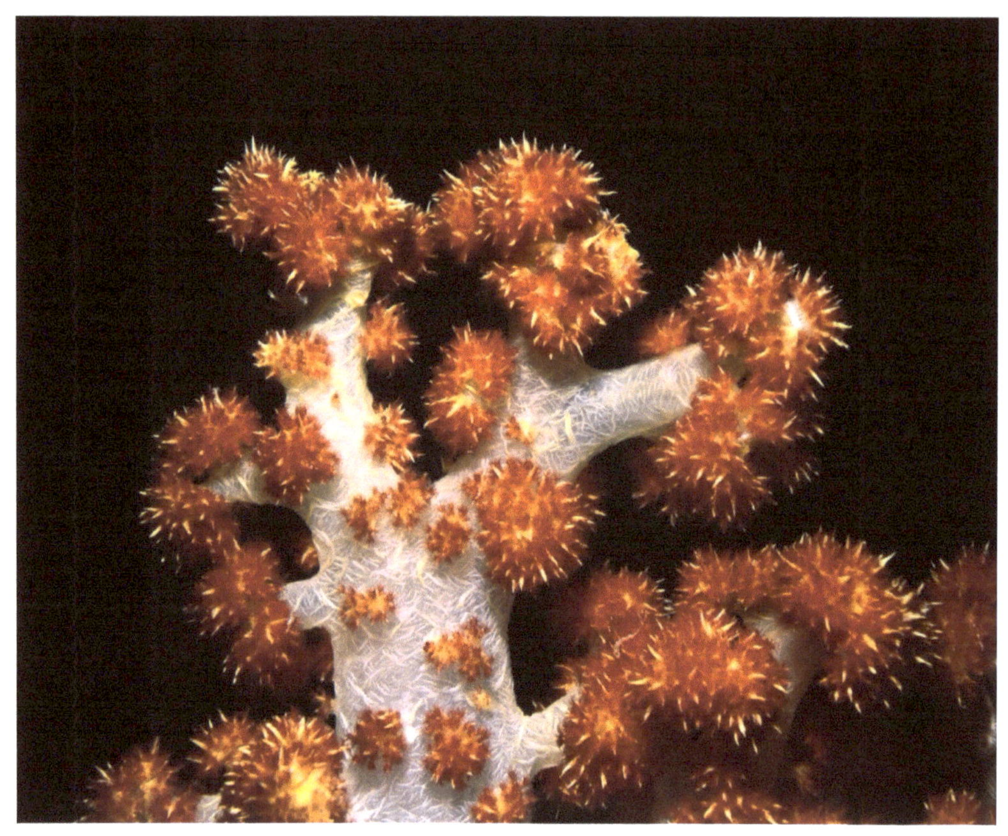

Neptheid

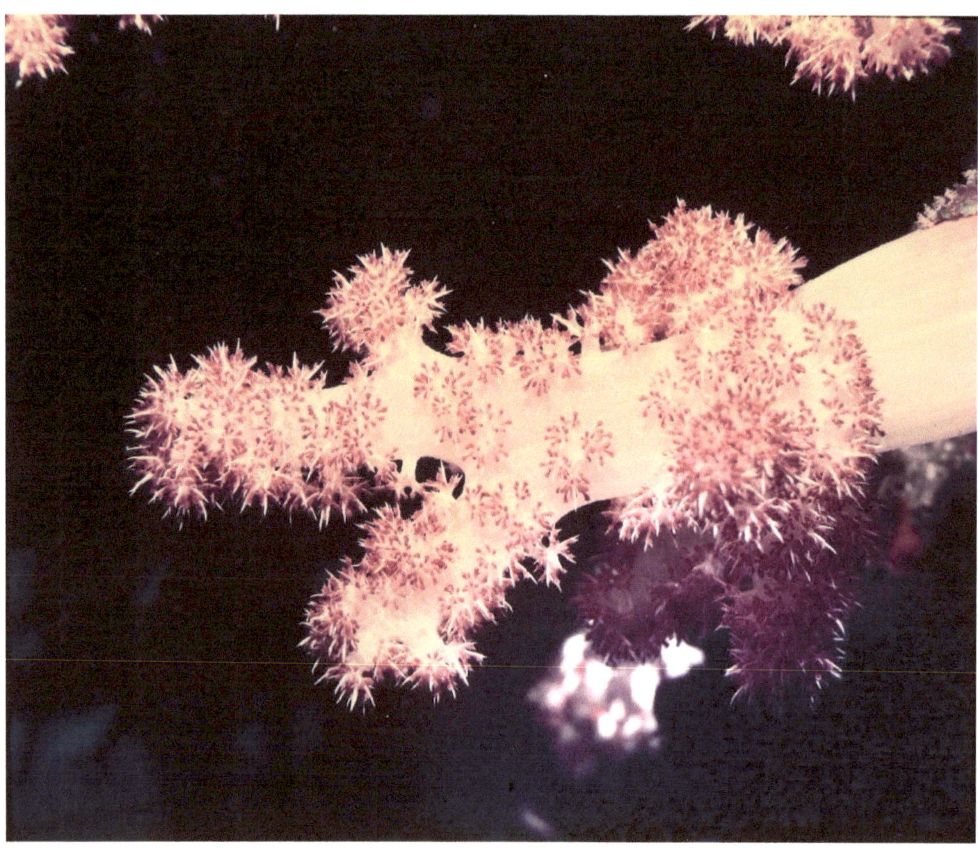

Neptheid

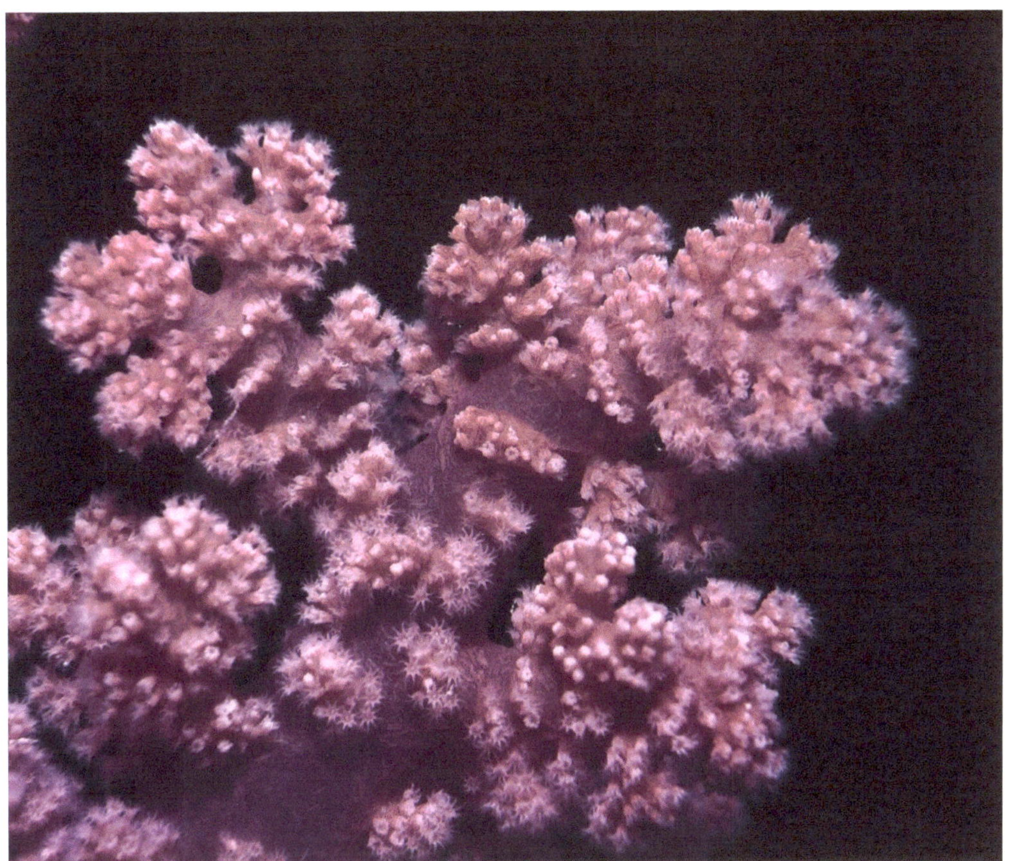

Gorgonid

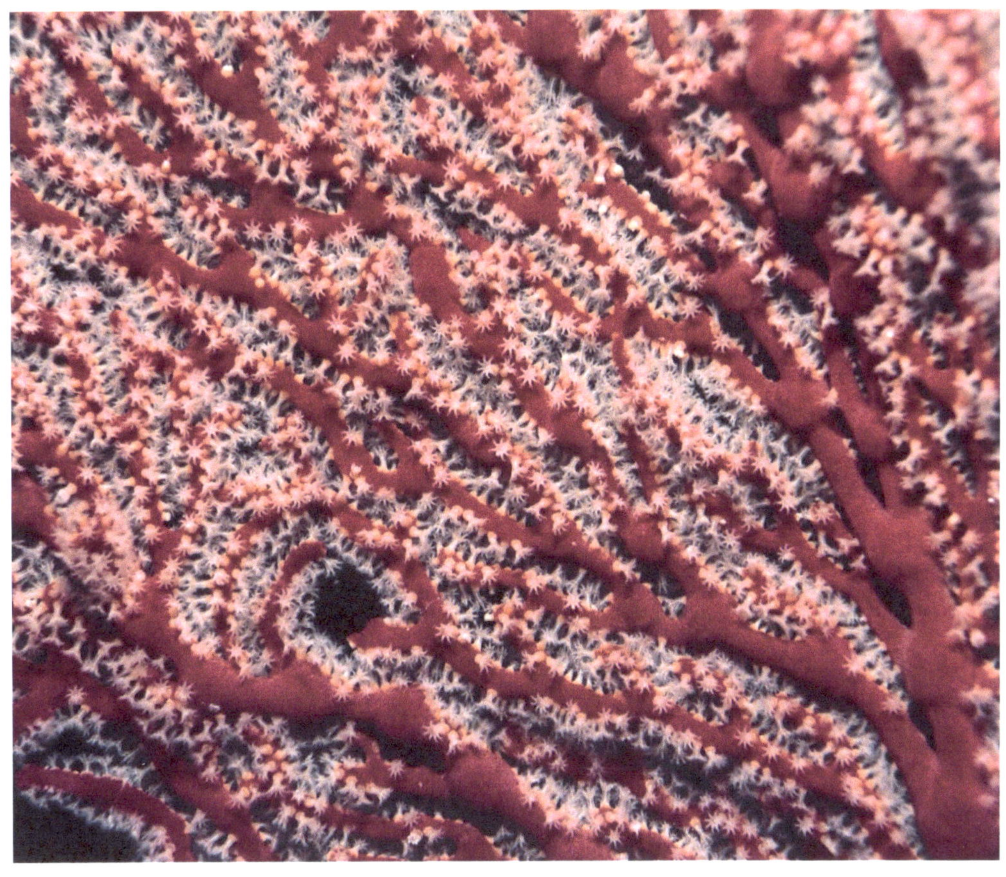

Gorgonid

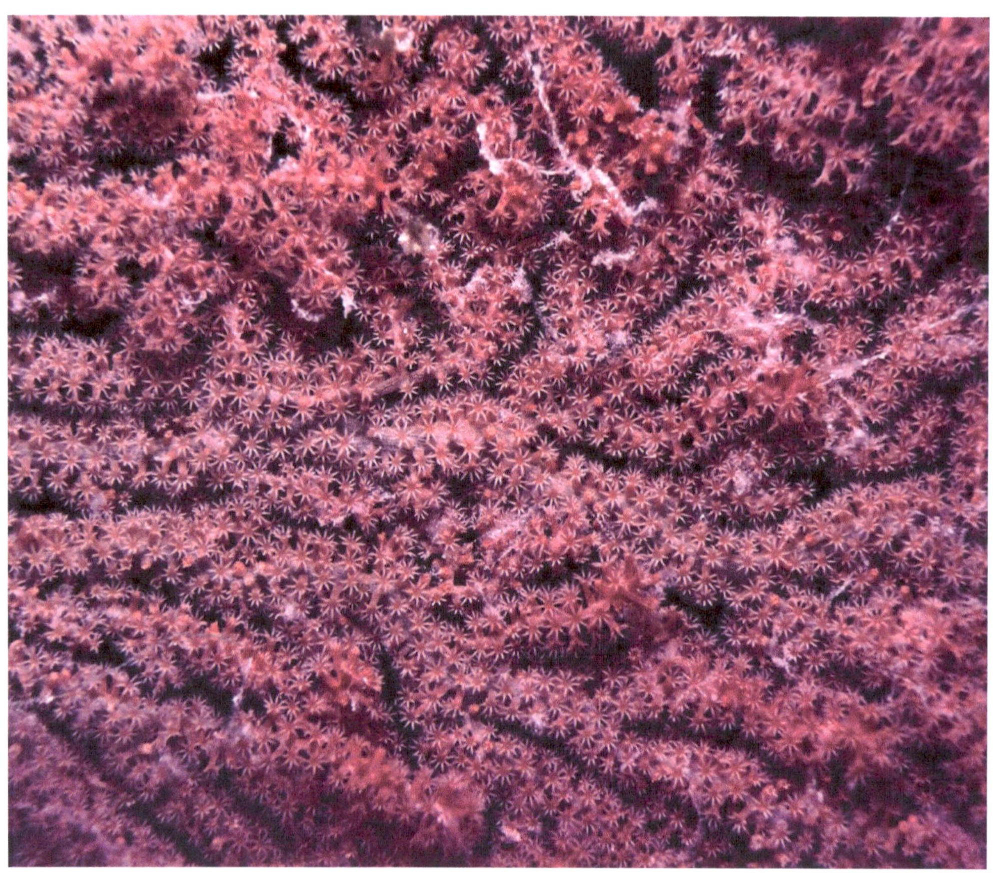

Penatulid (Sea Pen)

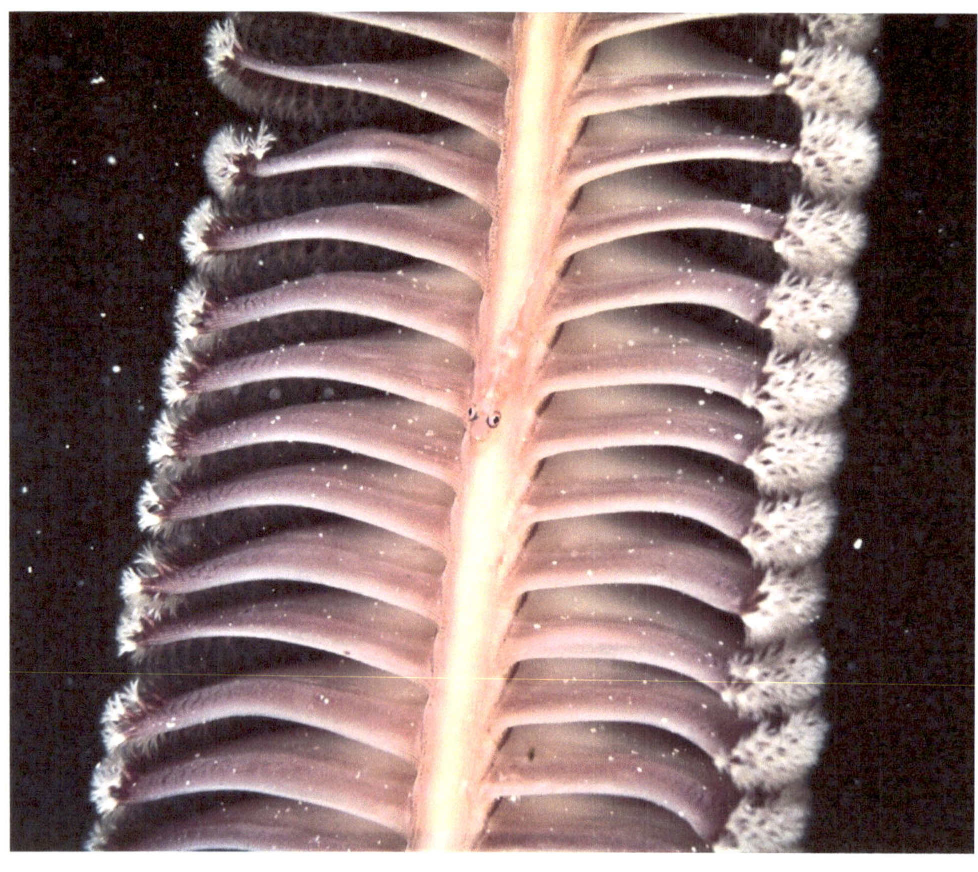

Hard Corals

Dendrophyllia sp.

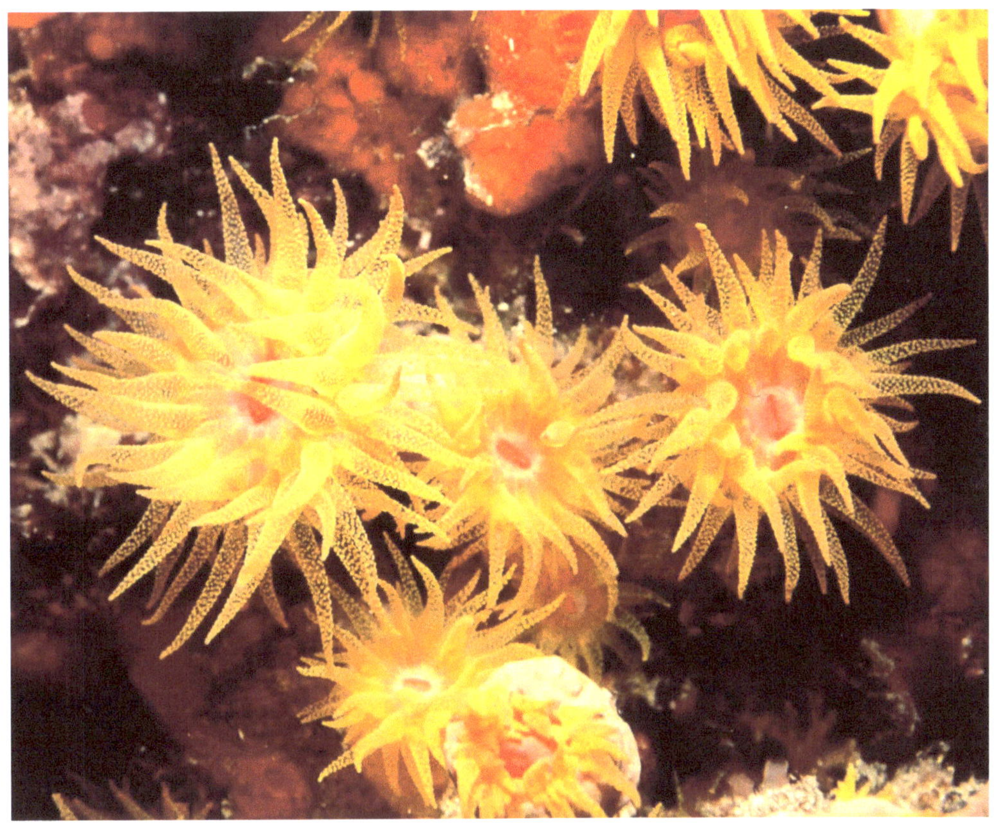

Pocilloporid

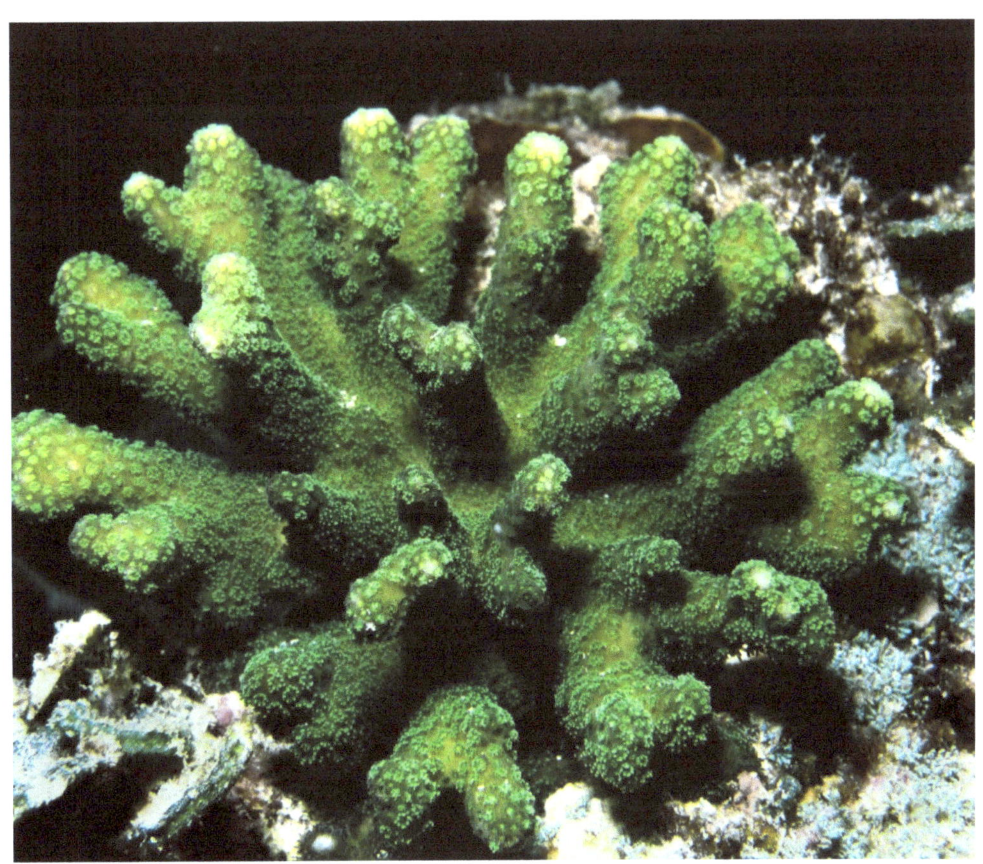

Pocilloporid

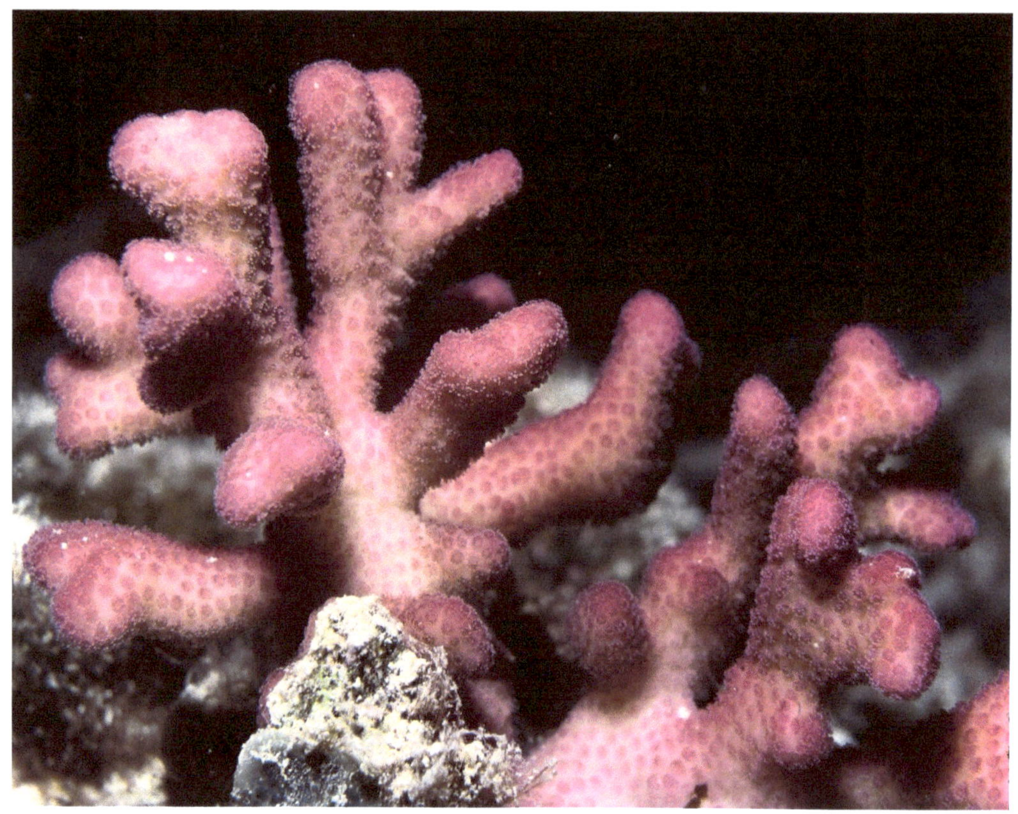

Fungid

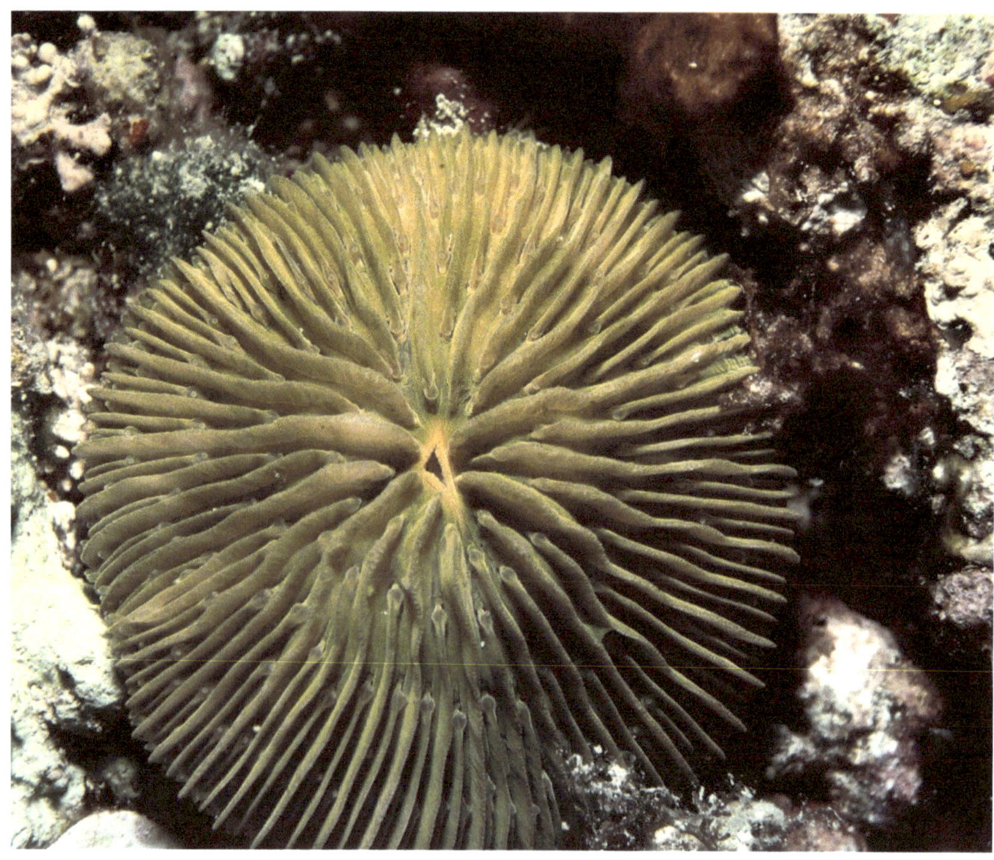

Mussid

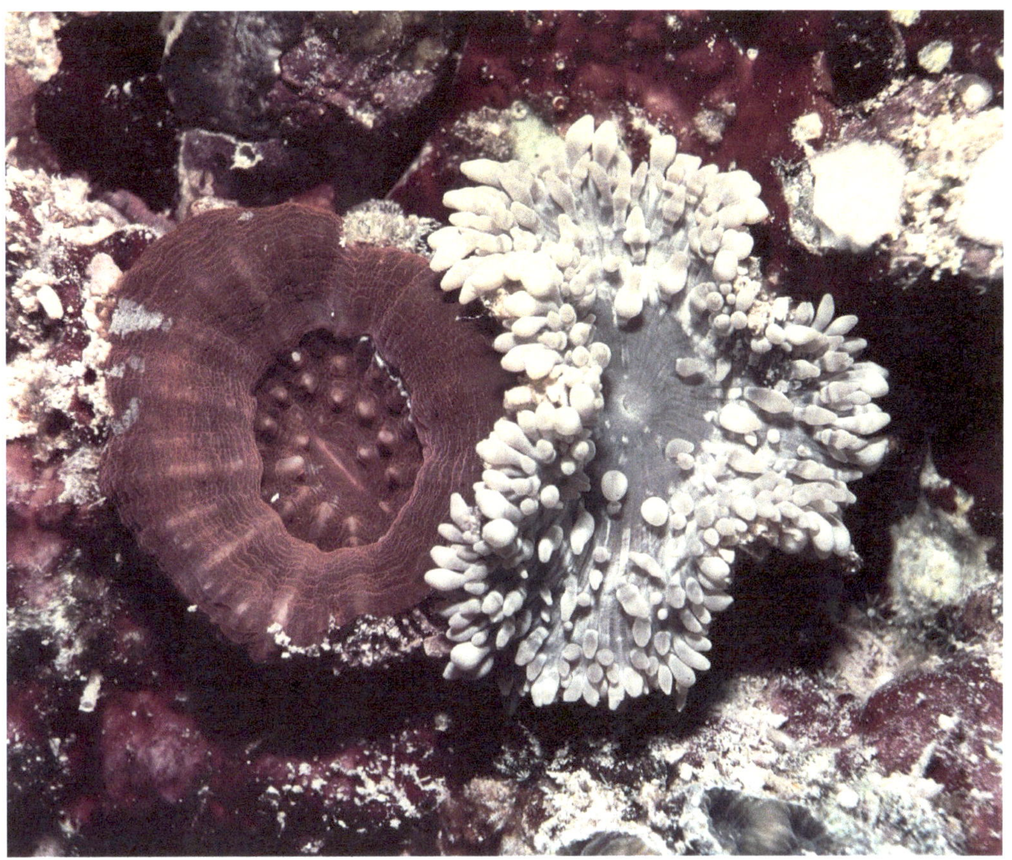

Mycedium sp.

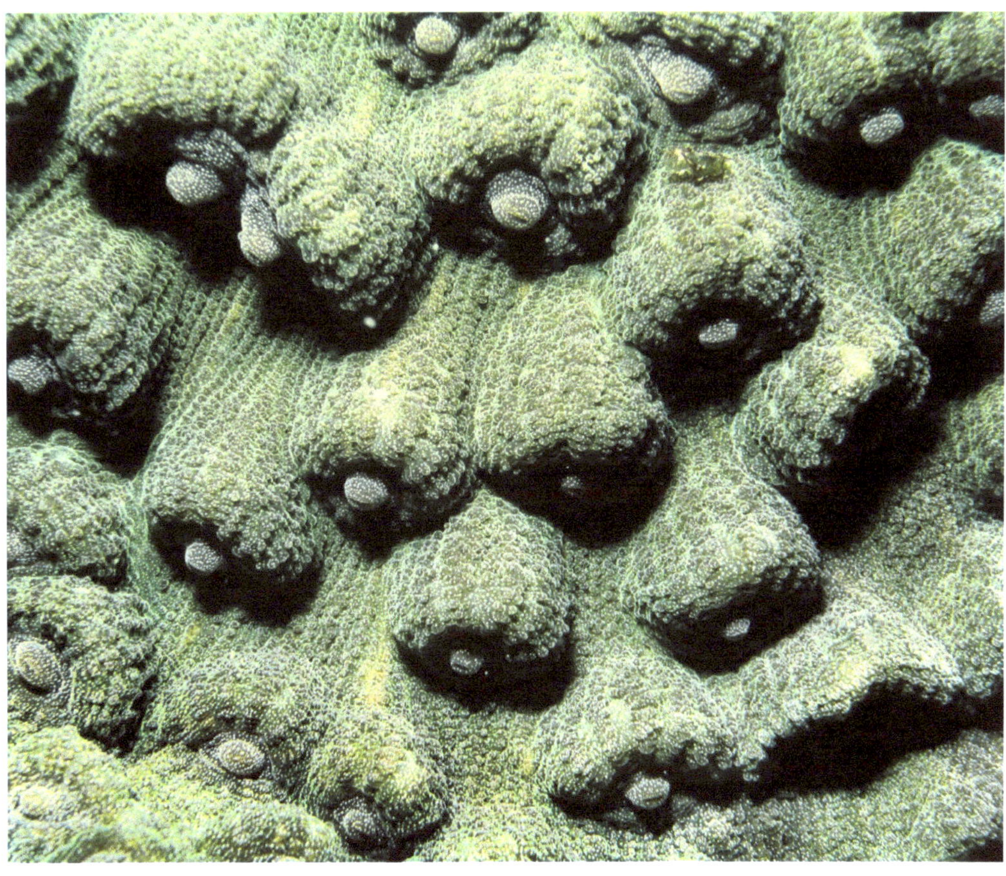

Worms

Protula magnifica

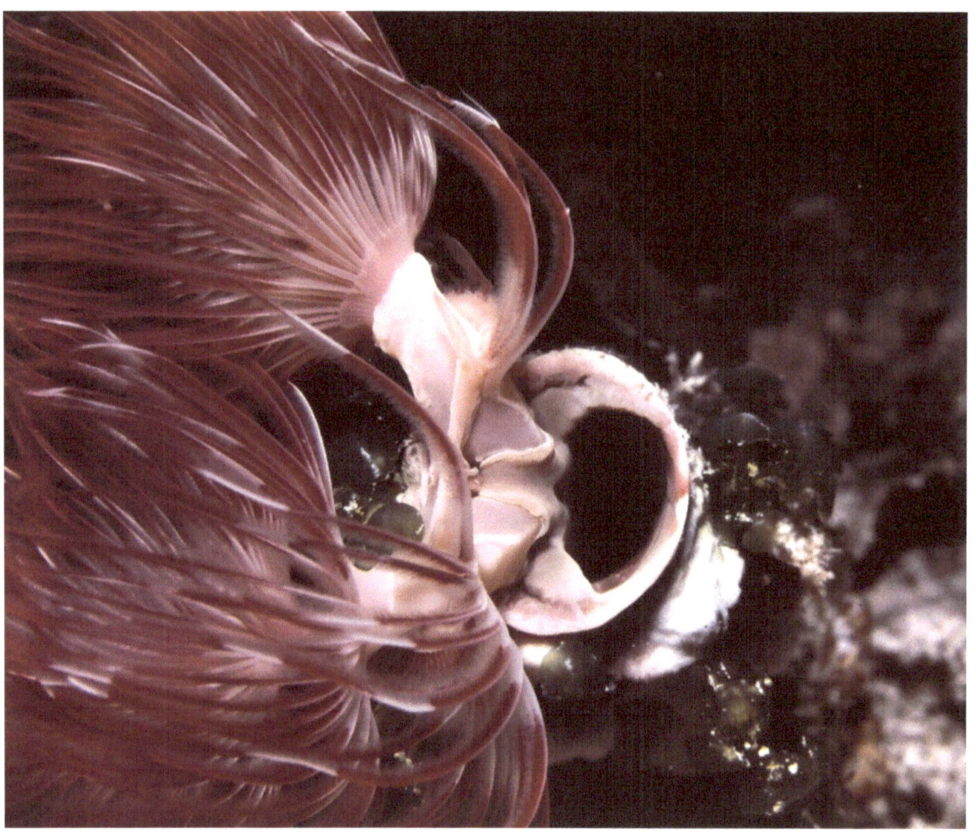

Spirobranchus sp.

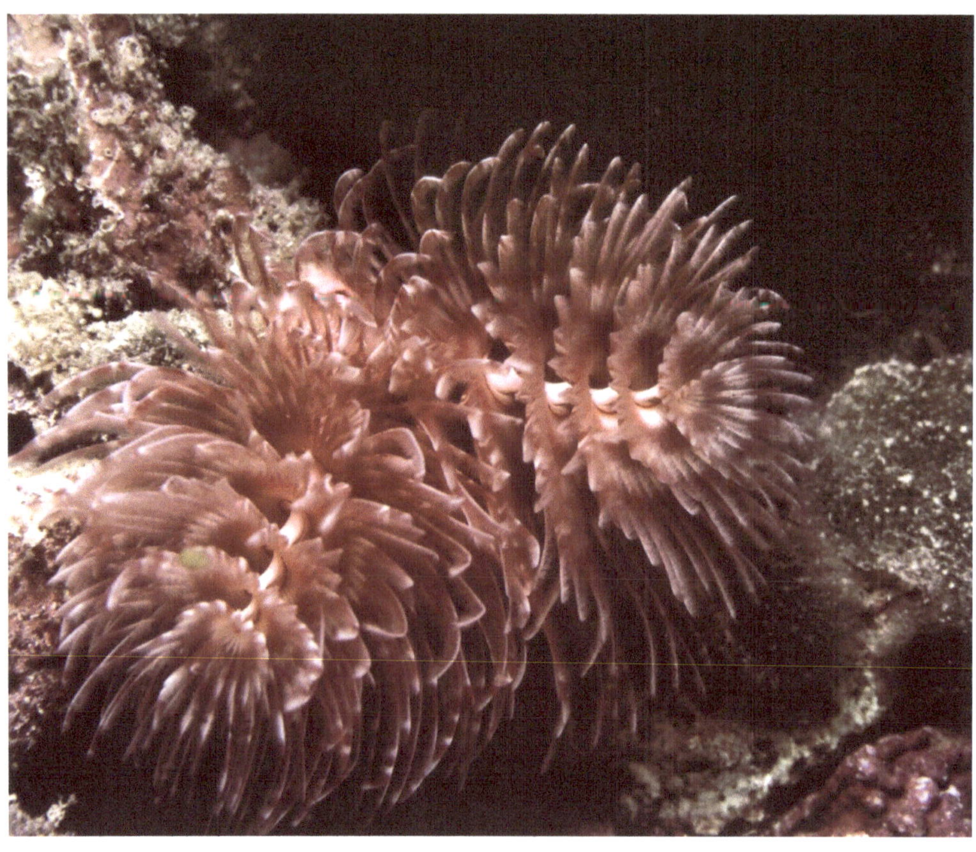

Molluscs

Tridacna sp.

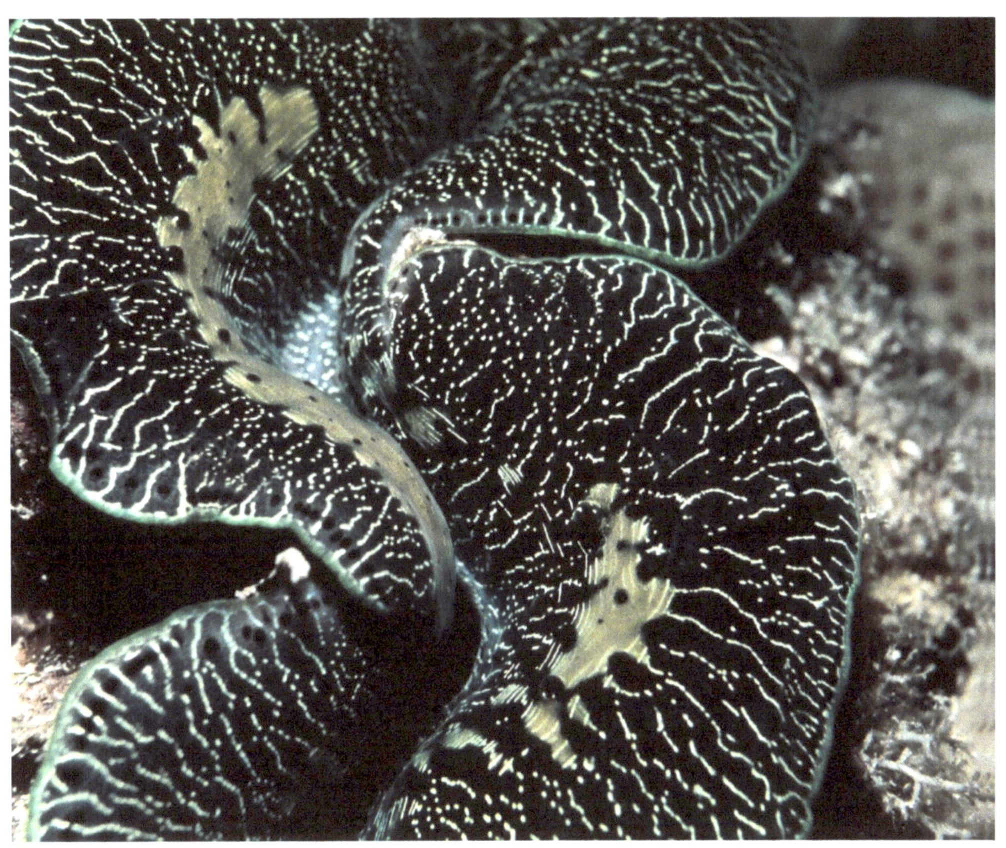

Lopha christagalli with worm tubes

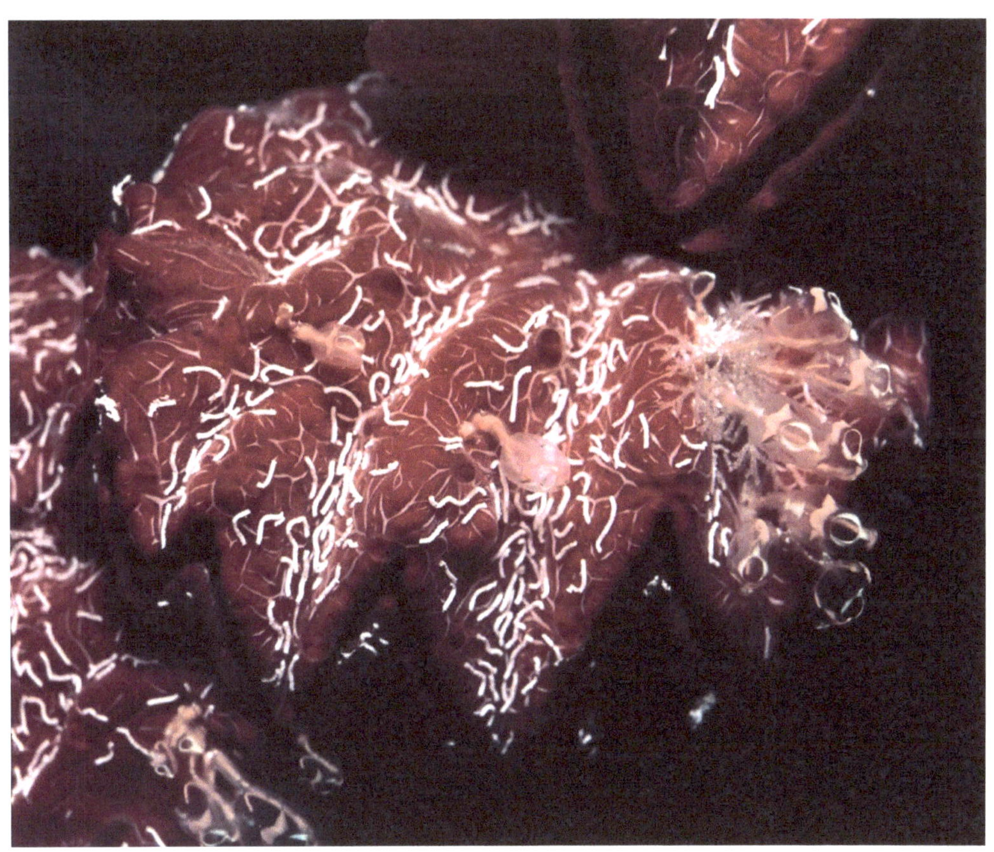

Nudibranch

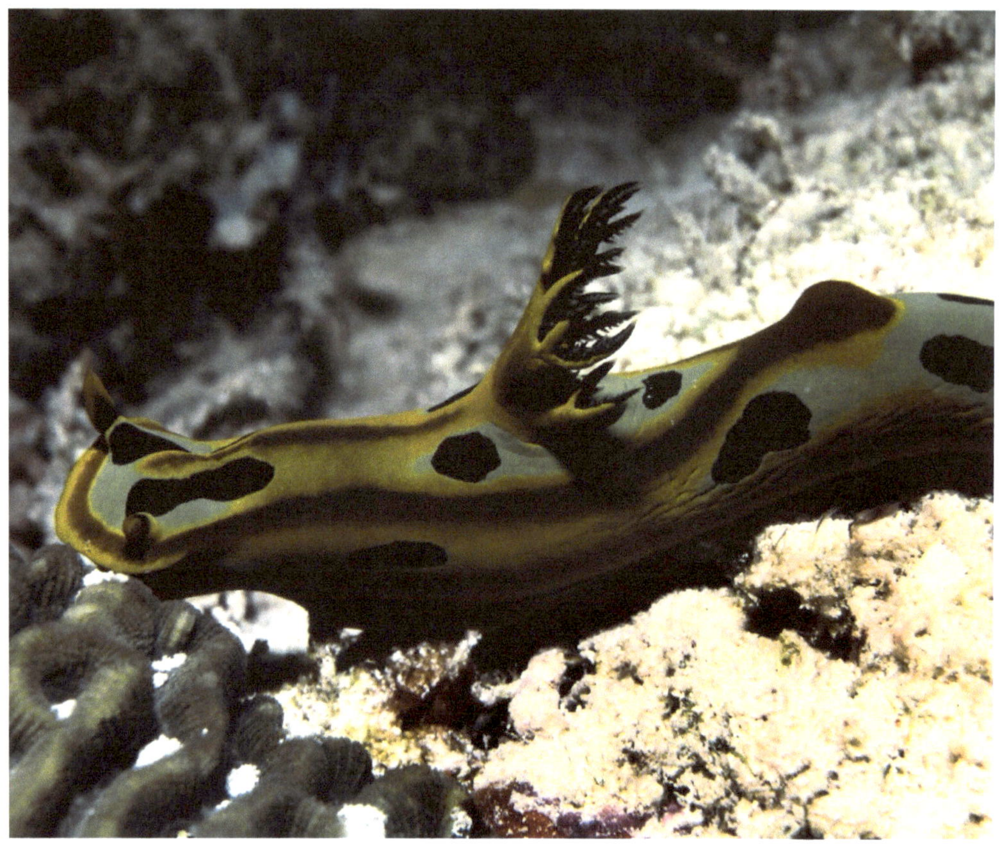

Aeolid

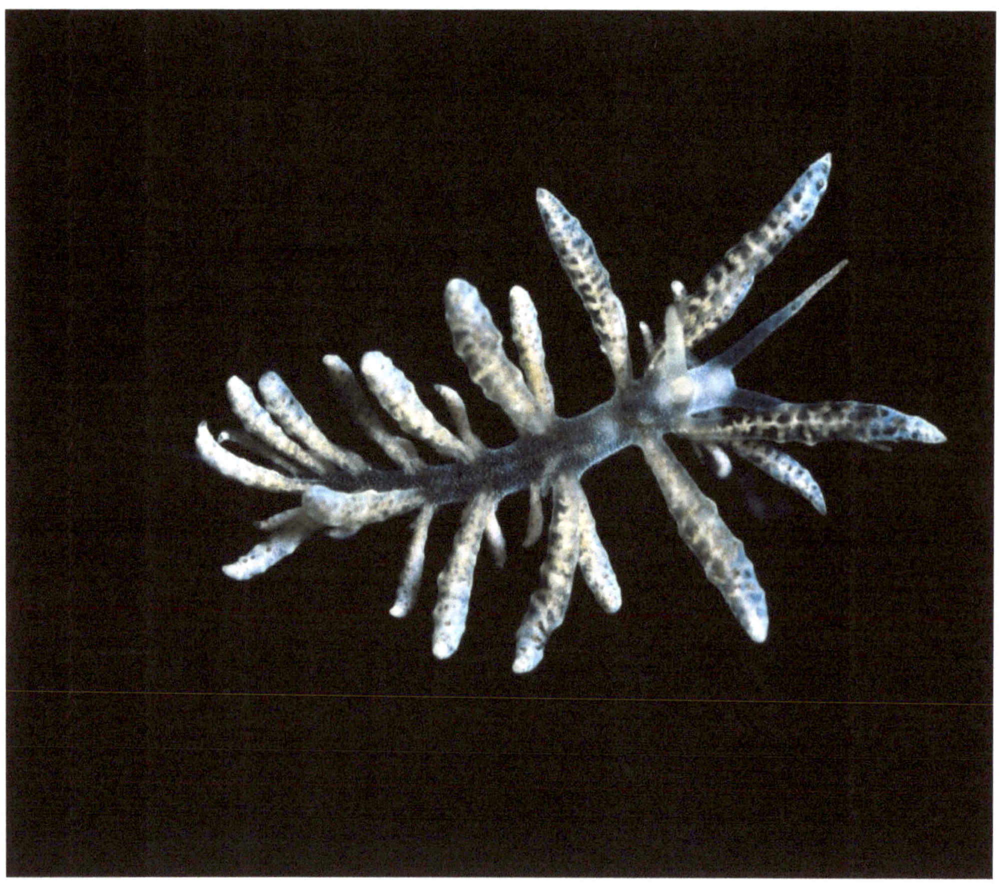

Crustacea

Shrimp

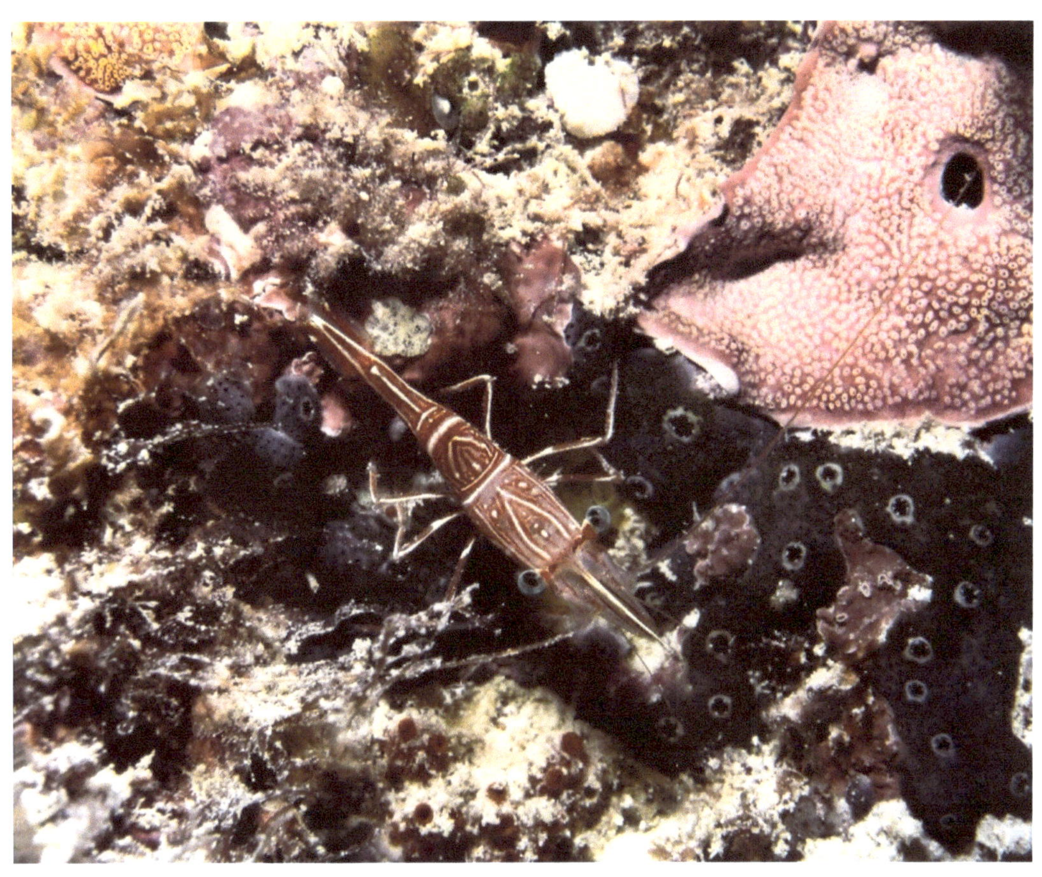

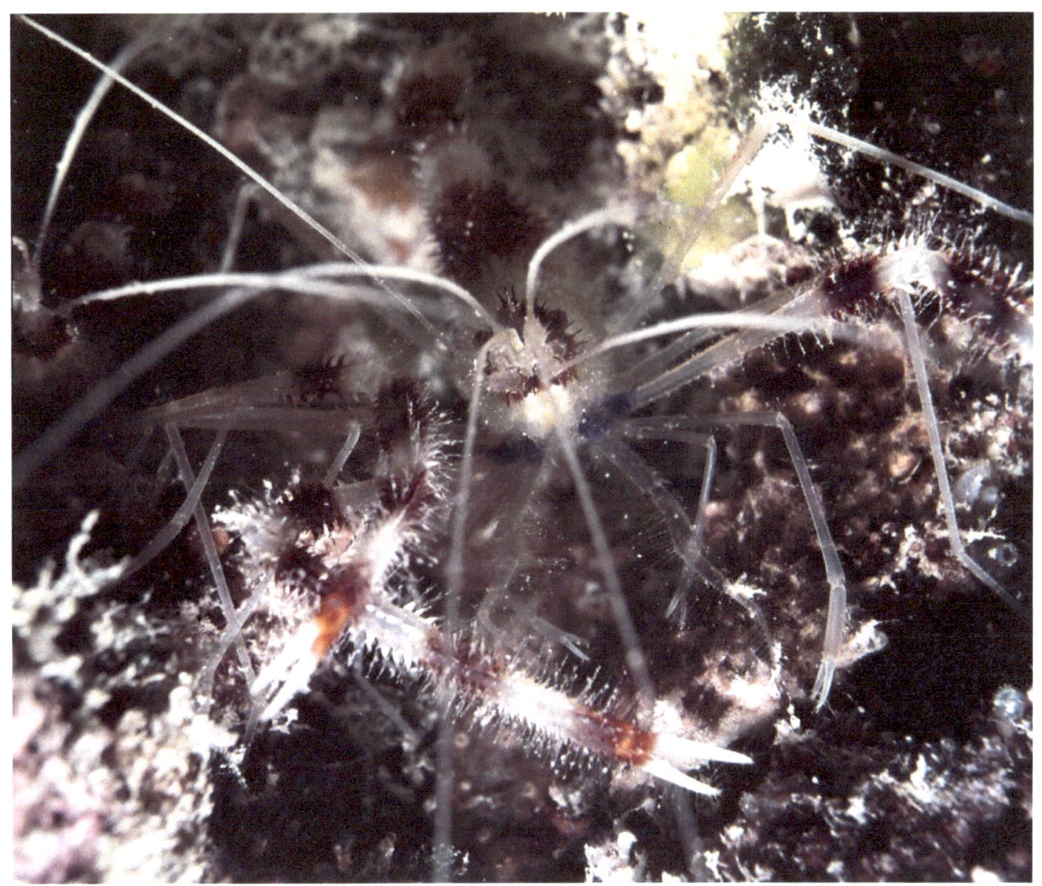

Starfish

Acanthaster planci

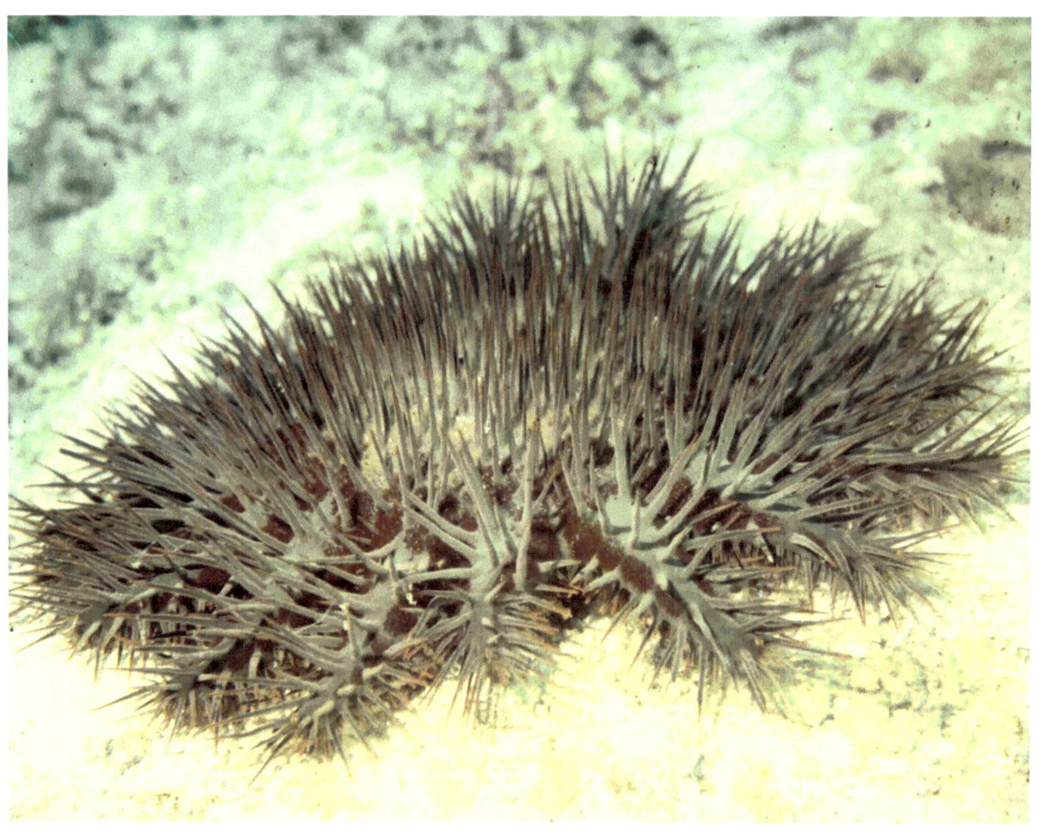

Acanthaster planci (close up)

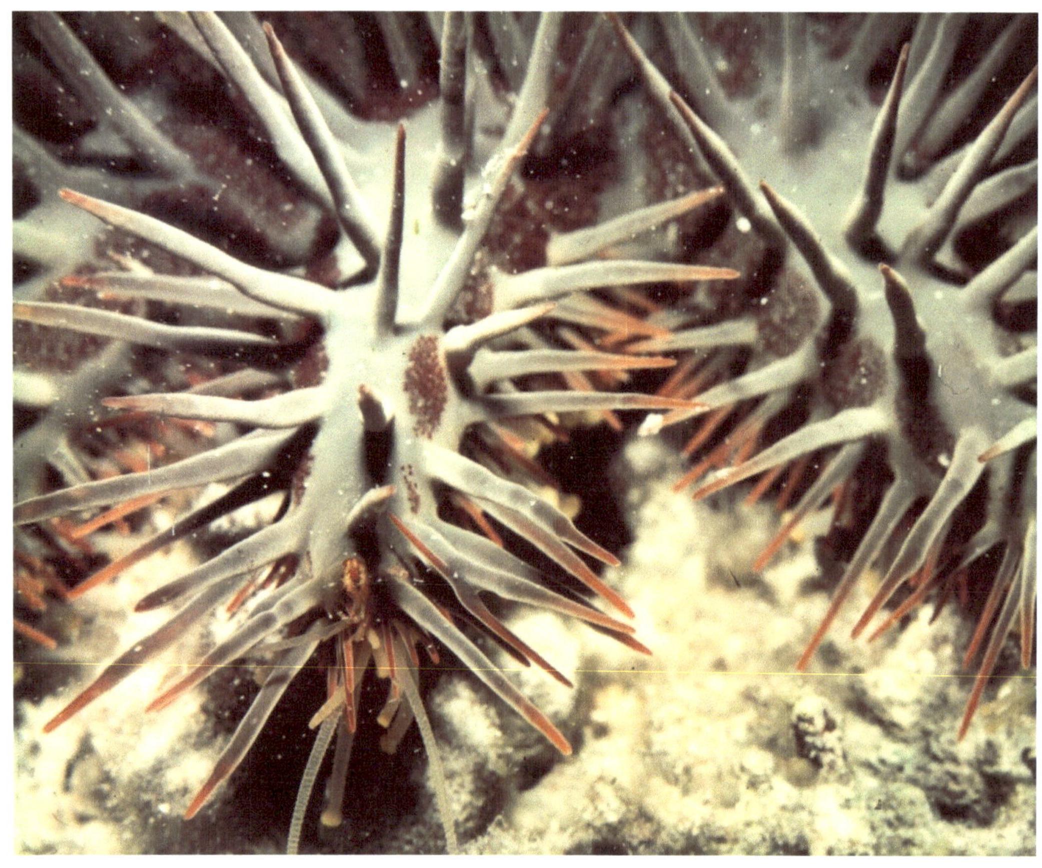

Euretaster insignis

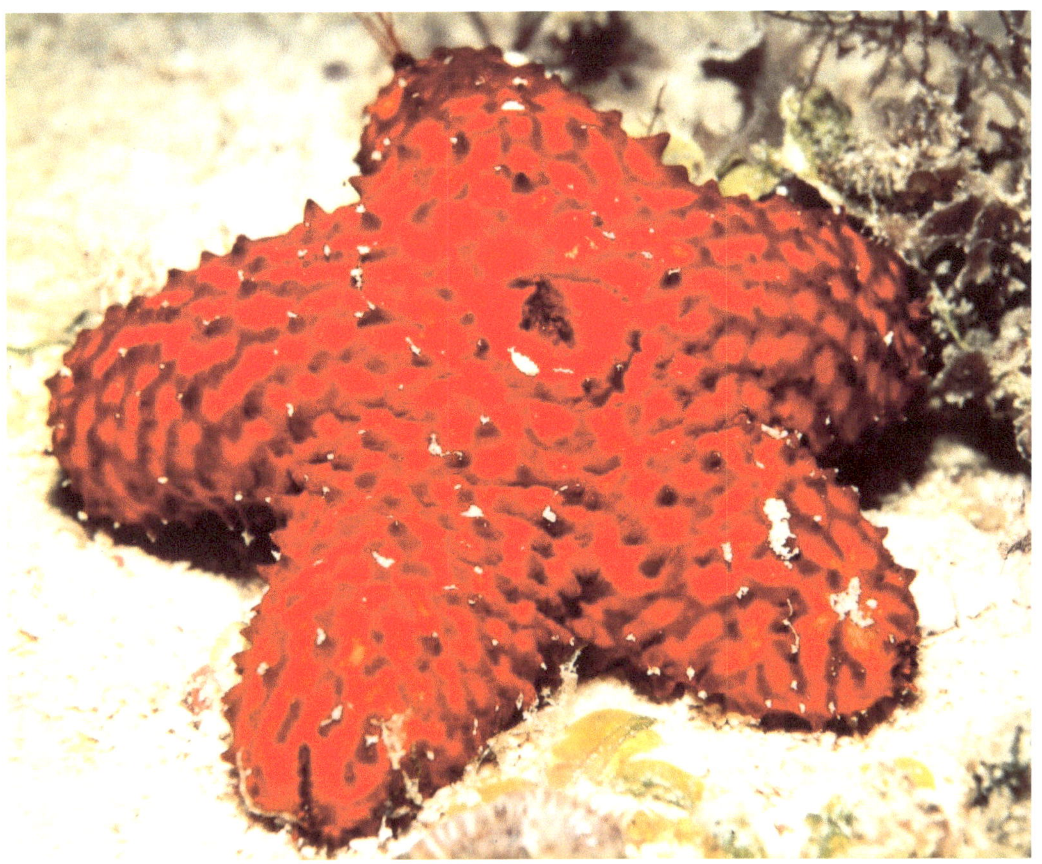

Ophidiaster robillardi

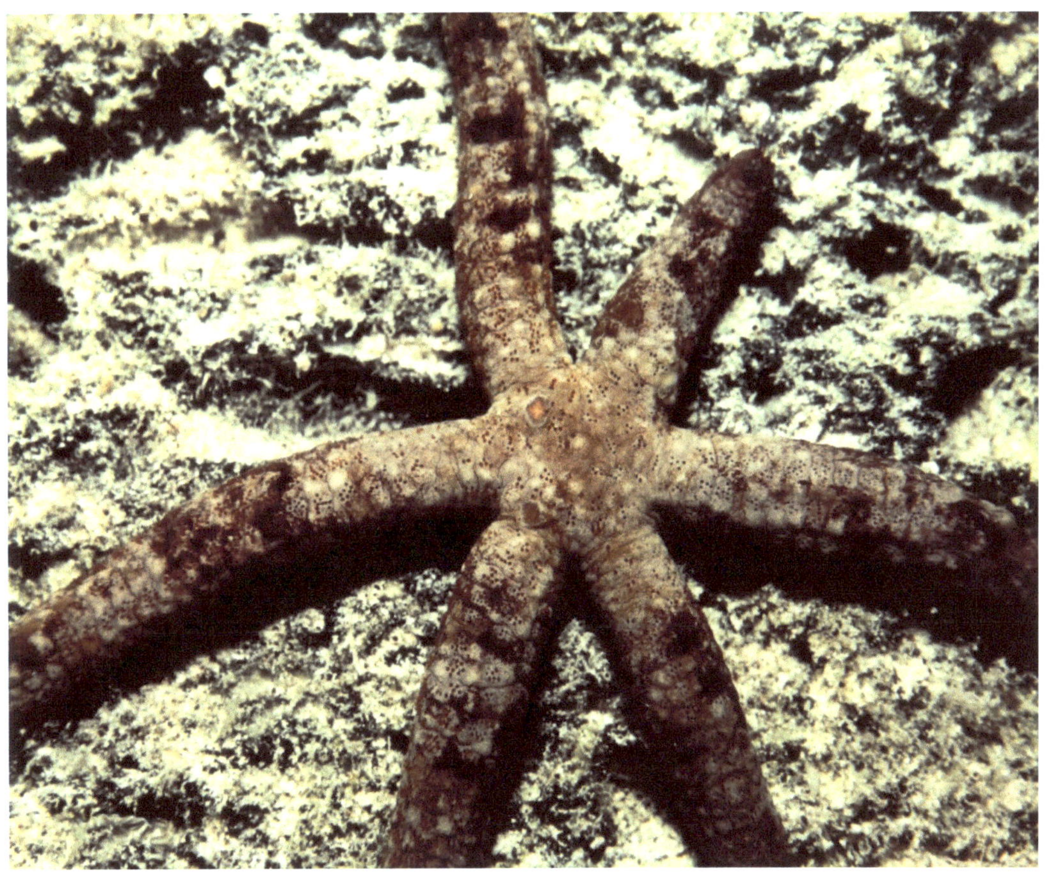

Fromia elegans

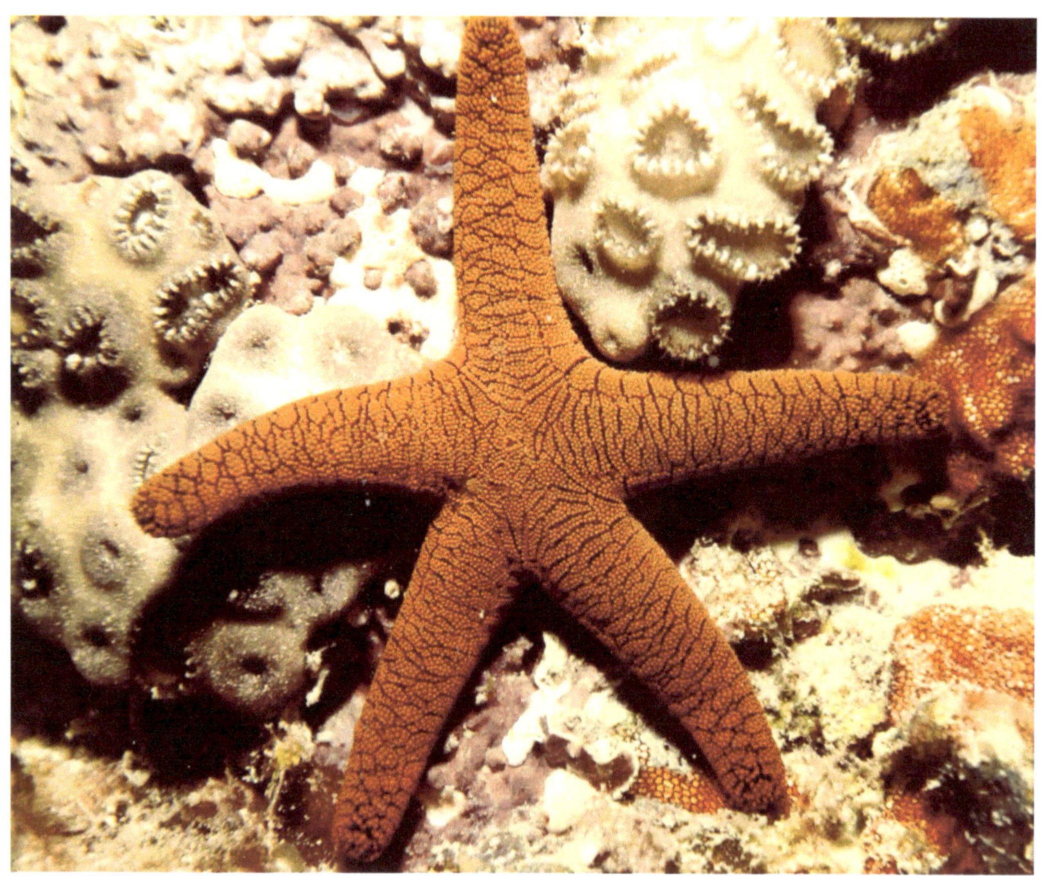

Echinaster luzonicus

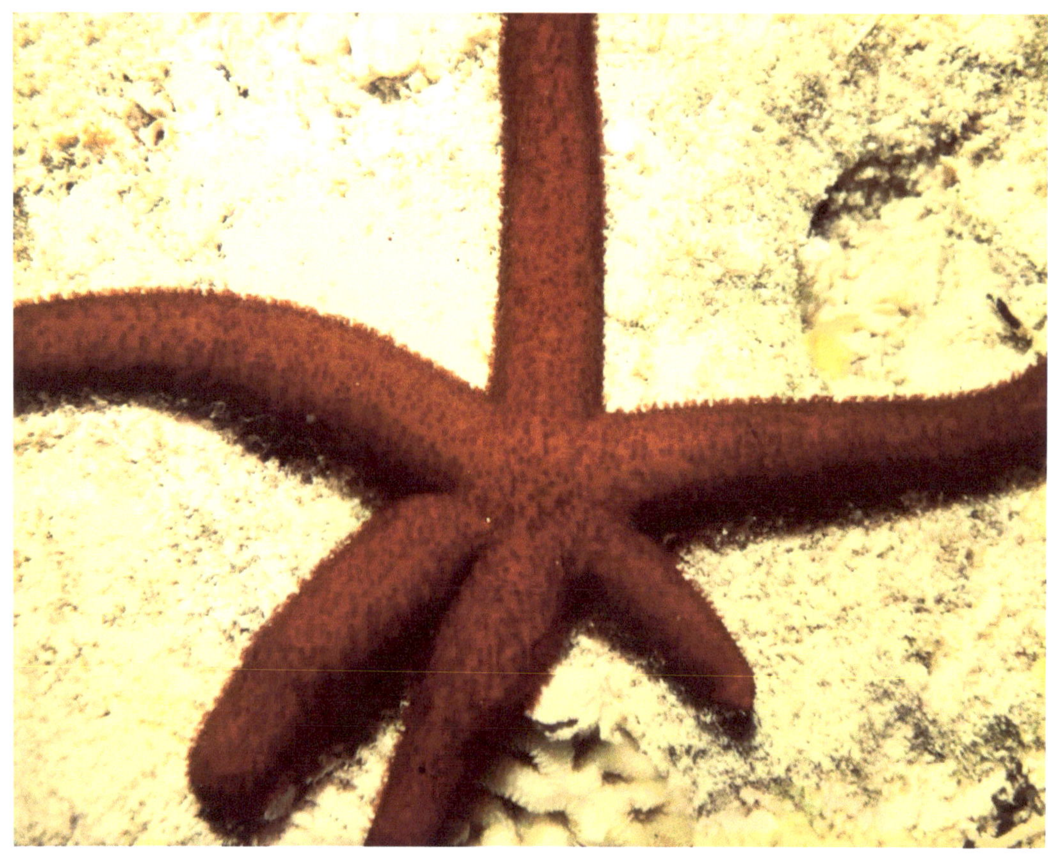

Ascidians

Pycnoclavella detorta

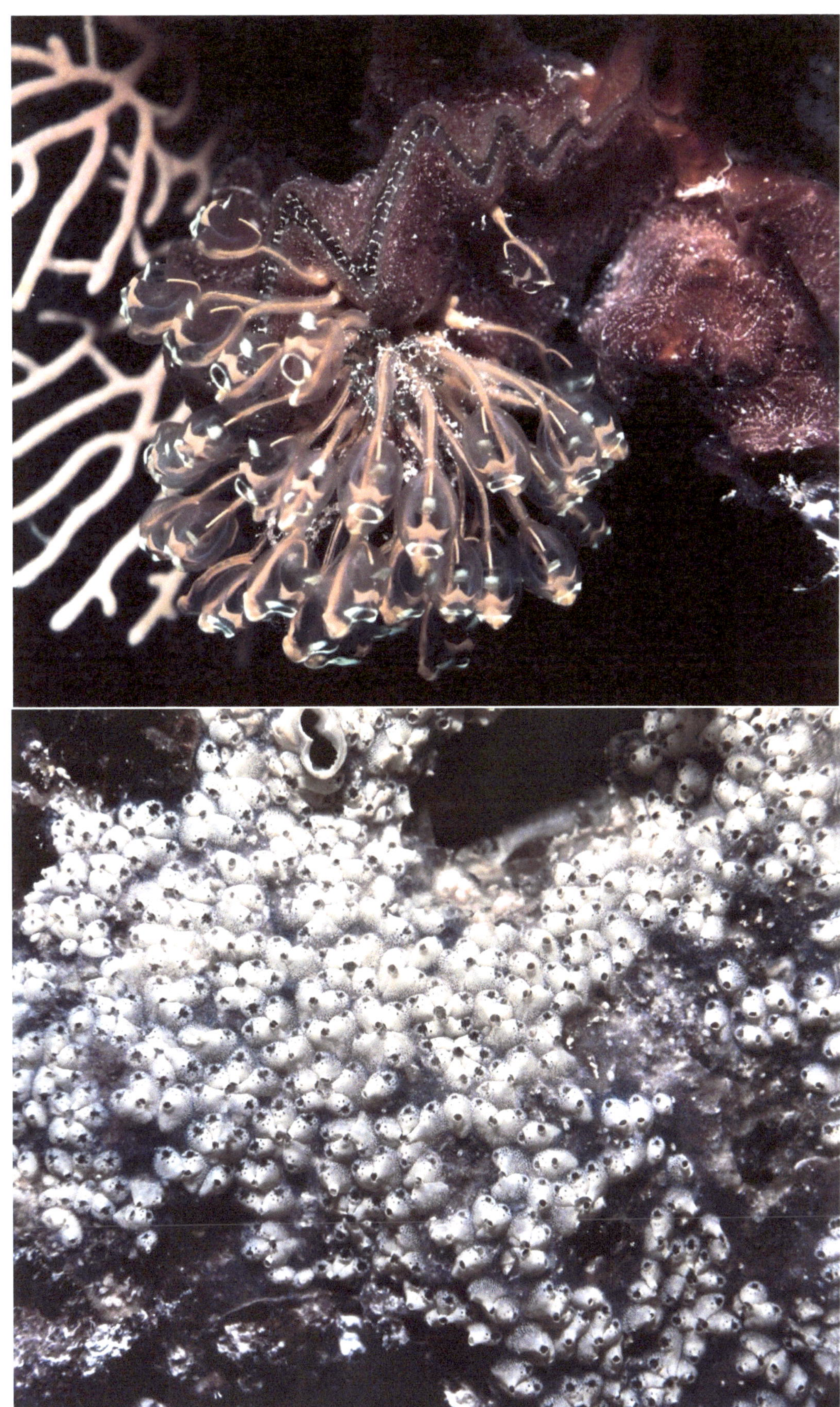

Fish

Blue Angel Fish

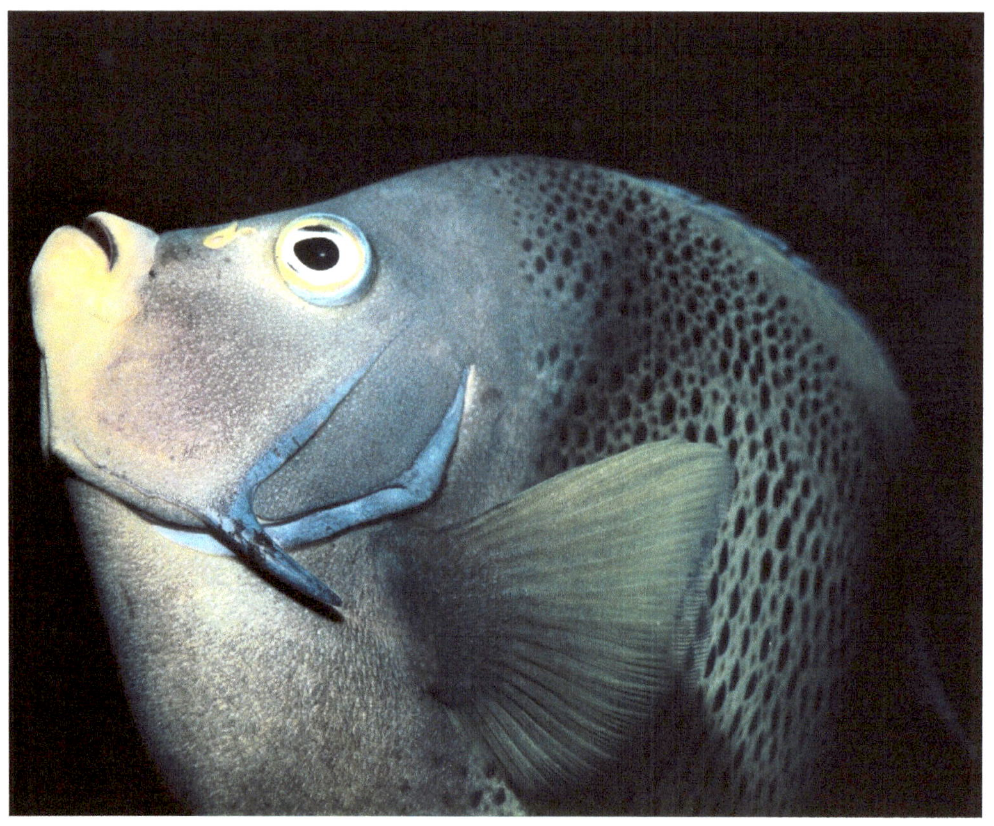

Coral Trout

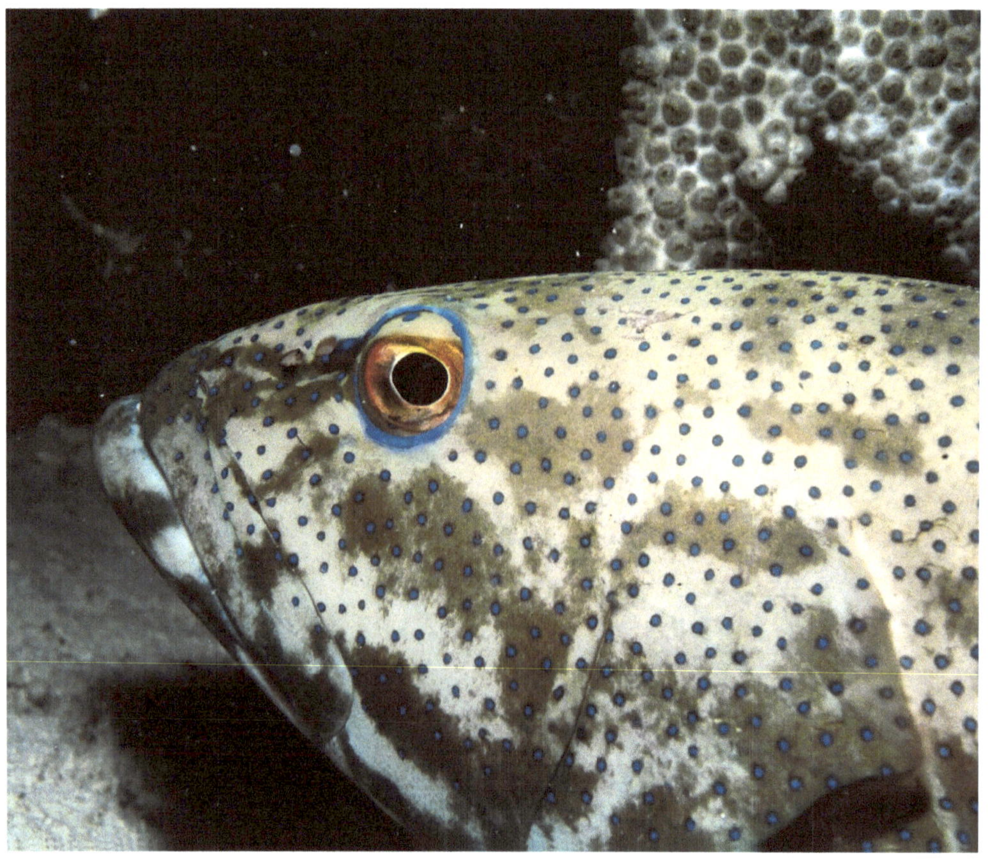

Rabbit Fish

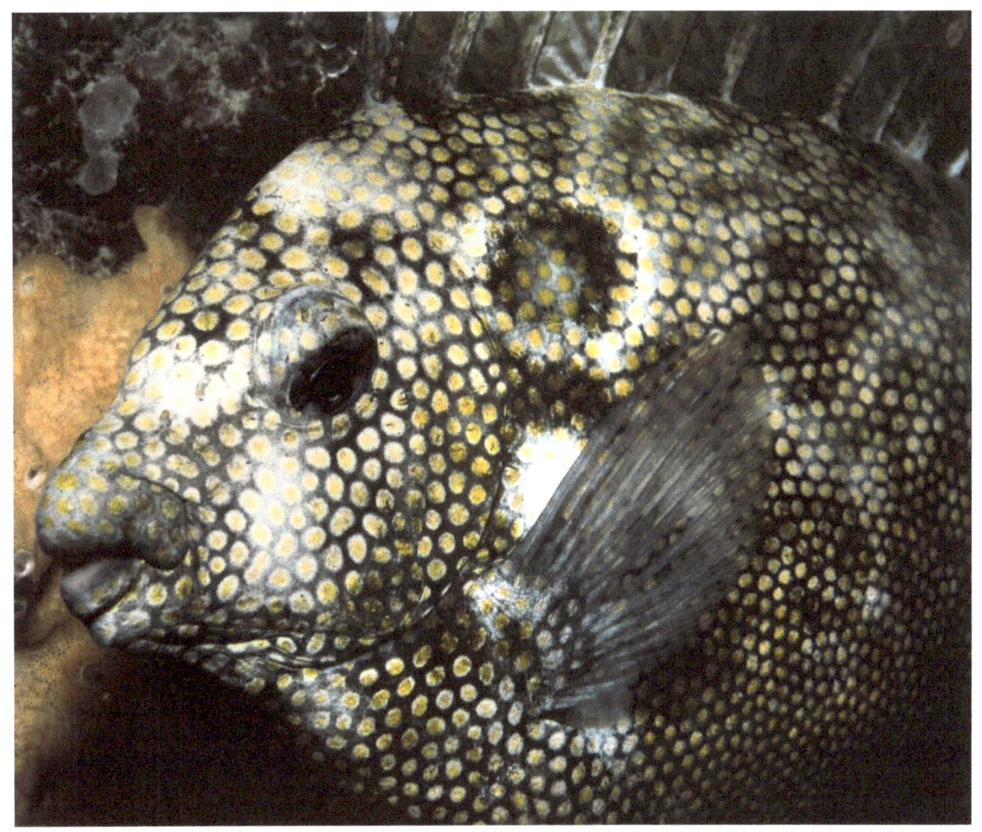

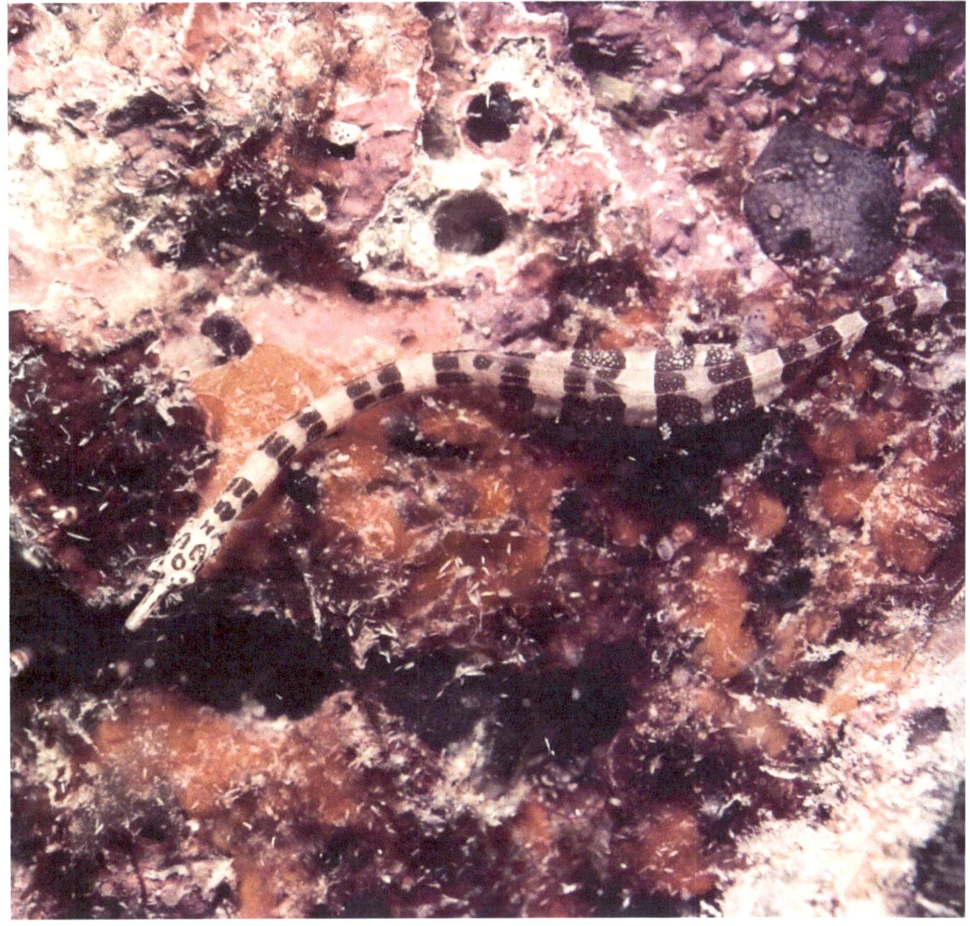

Green Island and Upolu Cay

Green Island (1971)

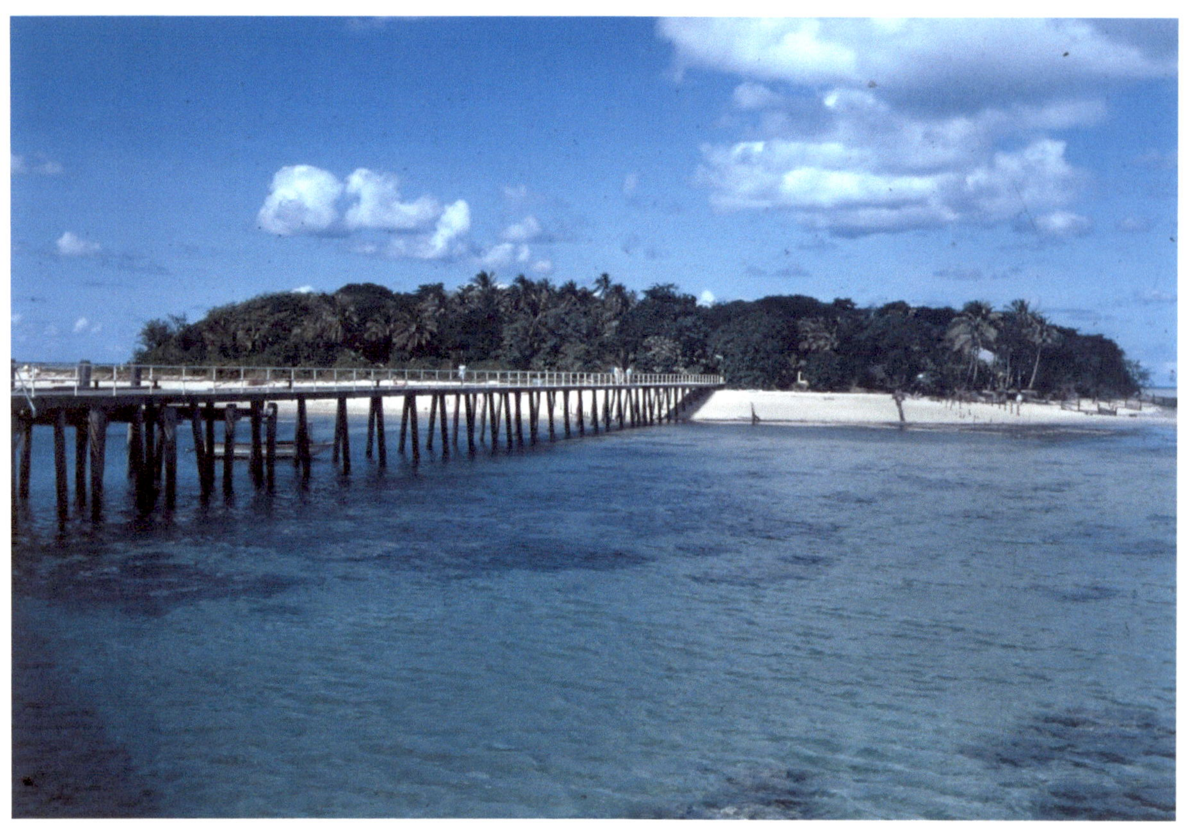

Green Island Jetty (1971)

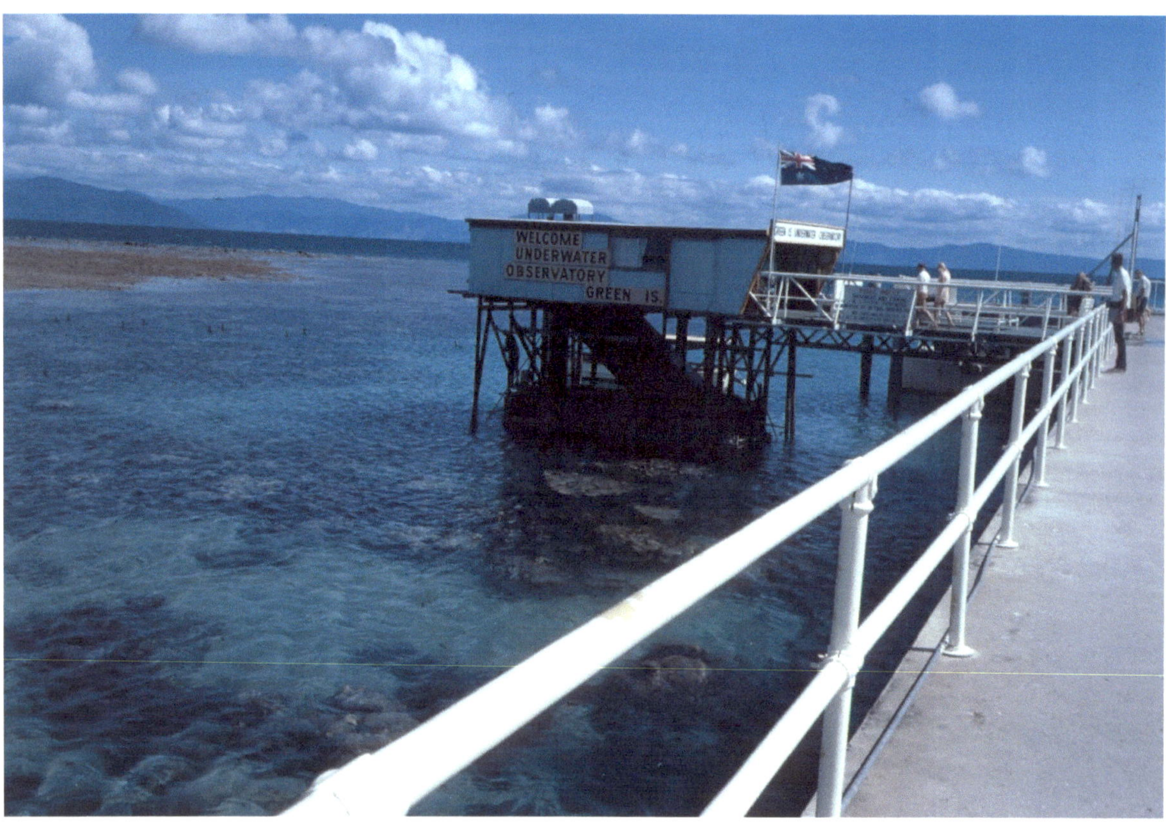

Green Island at low tide (1971)

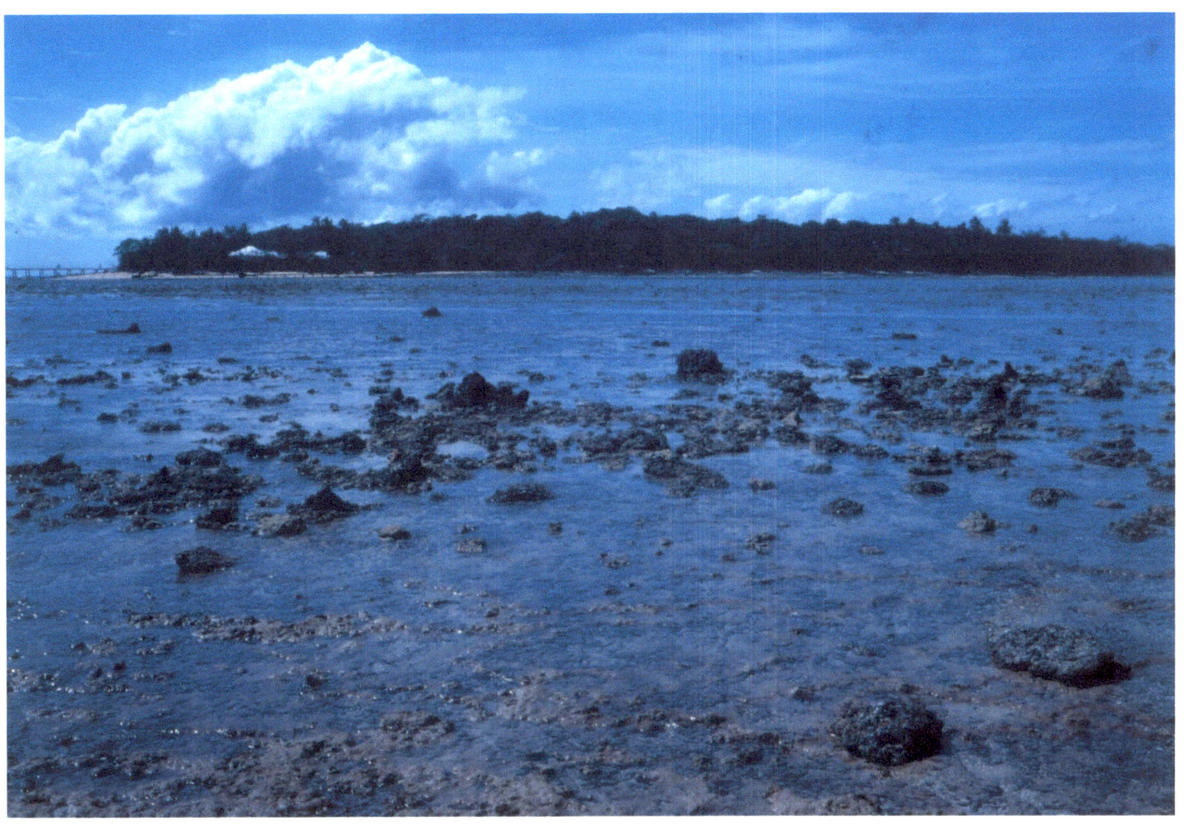

Upolu Cay (1971)

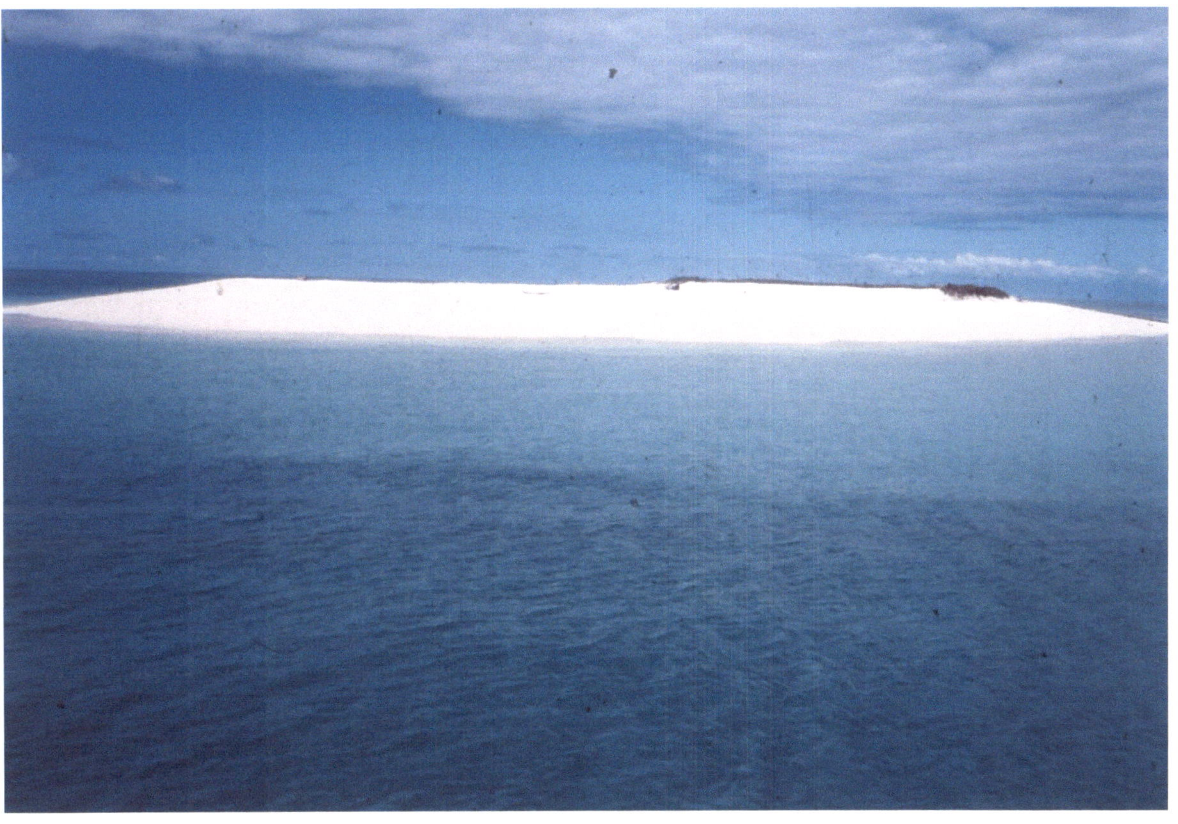

Upolu Cay (1971)

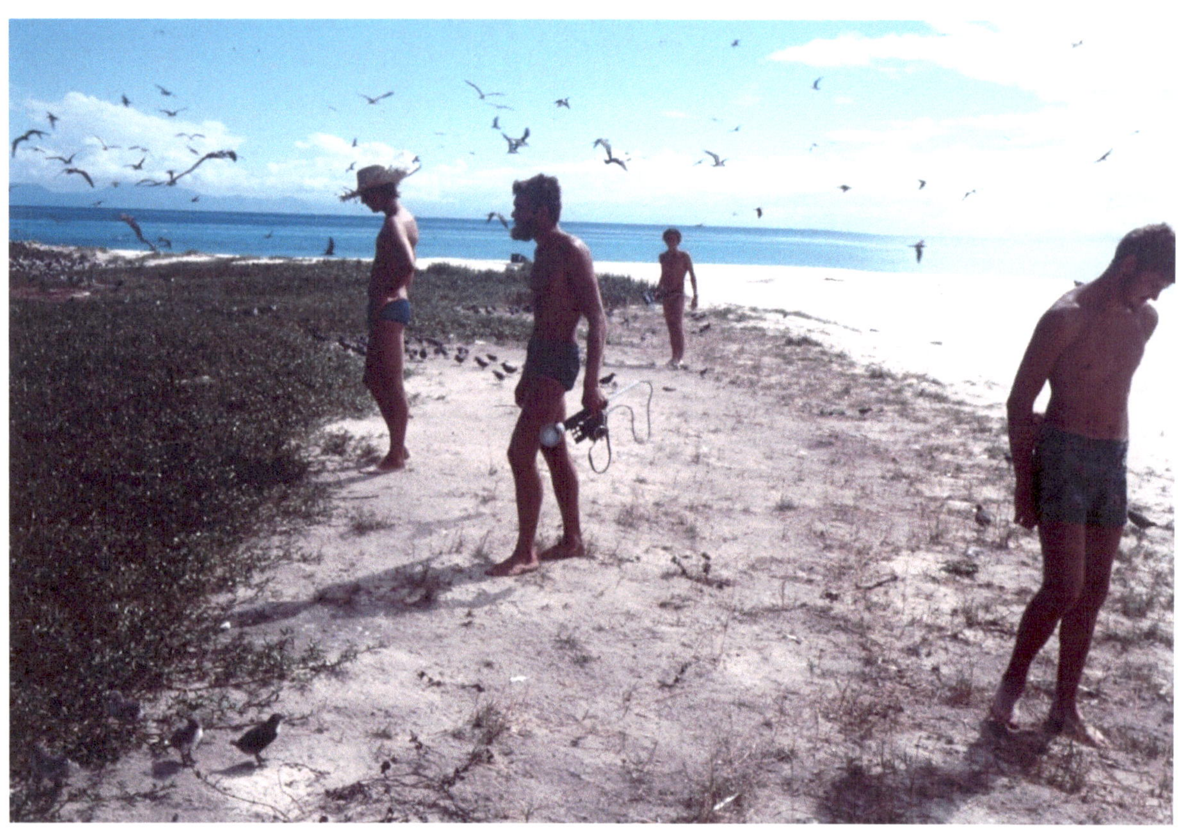

Crested Terns at Upolu Cay (1971)

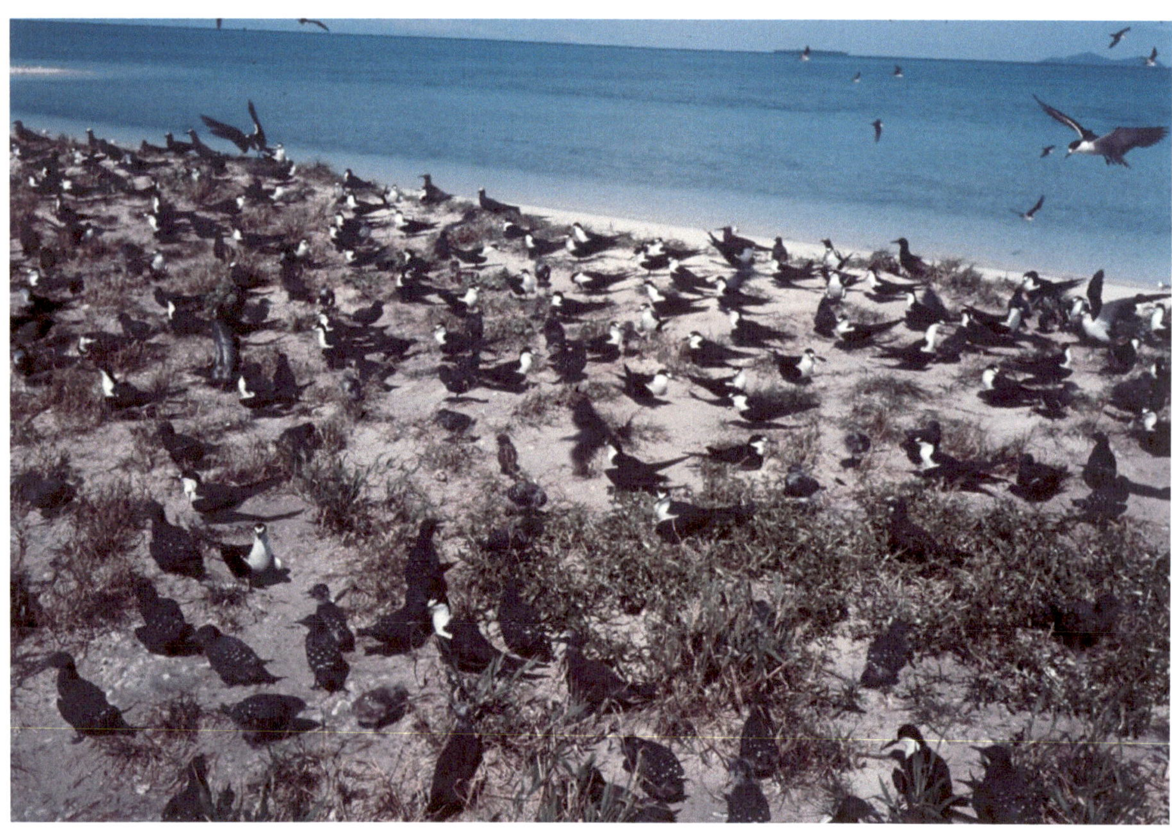

The future of the Great Barrier Reef

Since the late 1950's, coral reefs of the Indo-West Pacific region have experienced population outbreaks of the corallivorous crown-of-thorns starfish. The resultant loss of hard coral cover on some reefs of the Great Barrier Reef was studied during the period of outbreak, and subsequently, so that both the short- and long-term effects of this predator would be known.

The role of this predator in the elevation or lowering of coral species diversity on the Great Barrier Reef has not been studied adequately. It is apparent that some reefs become reinfested with starfish about 15 years following the initial infestation. It would appear, that when the quantity (not necessarily diversity) of a reef's hard coral cover has regrown, the starfish can recruit again in high numbers.

Although the COTS outbreak phenomenon has puzzled scientists for a quarter of a century, and although many explanatory hypotheses and models have been proposed, there remains disagreement about the causes of the phenomenon. Additionally, there is disagreement about the need for reef management strategies, that might mitigate the widespread effects of this coral predator.

The extent of present population outbreaks, and the possibility of past outbreaks (prior to 1960) have not been studied in sufficient detail to allow critical evaluation of either the problem itself, or the risks associated with incorrect management. We do not know what factors allow high recruitment of this starfish on some reefs when, on other reefs, it maintains a low population density.

The natural life expectancy, larval dispersal, and adult migration of this starfish, while central to an understanding of the phenomenon, are not understood sufficiently. The role of natural predators in maintaining high diversity, and the possible survival strategy of rarity in the coral reef community have not been studied adequately.

Human collection of the Giant Triton and other predators was suggested by Endean (1969) as a causative factor in starfish outbreaks, but this Predator Control Hypothesis was generally disregarded due to the enormous potential numbers of starfish. Recent research demonstrating the strong avoidance reaction of the starfish to the triton together with an understanding of the importance of starfish aggregation to reproductive success may be slowly changing this opinion.

In addition to starfish outbreaks, the Great Barrier Reef is suffering from recurring coral bleaching events due to global warming and increased nutrient runoff from the adjacent mainland. It will require a sustained effort to understand the impact of these events and how best to mitigate them. In the end, the future of the Reef is up to us to decide.

The following Artificial Intelligence (AI) images are derived from the previous pictures using Dream Studio and show the enormous future potential of the Great Barrier Reef's beauty, whether it be related to conservation, ecotourism, or art.

Diver Dreaming

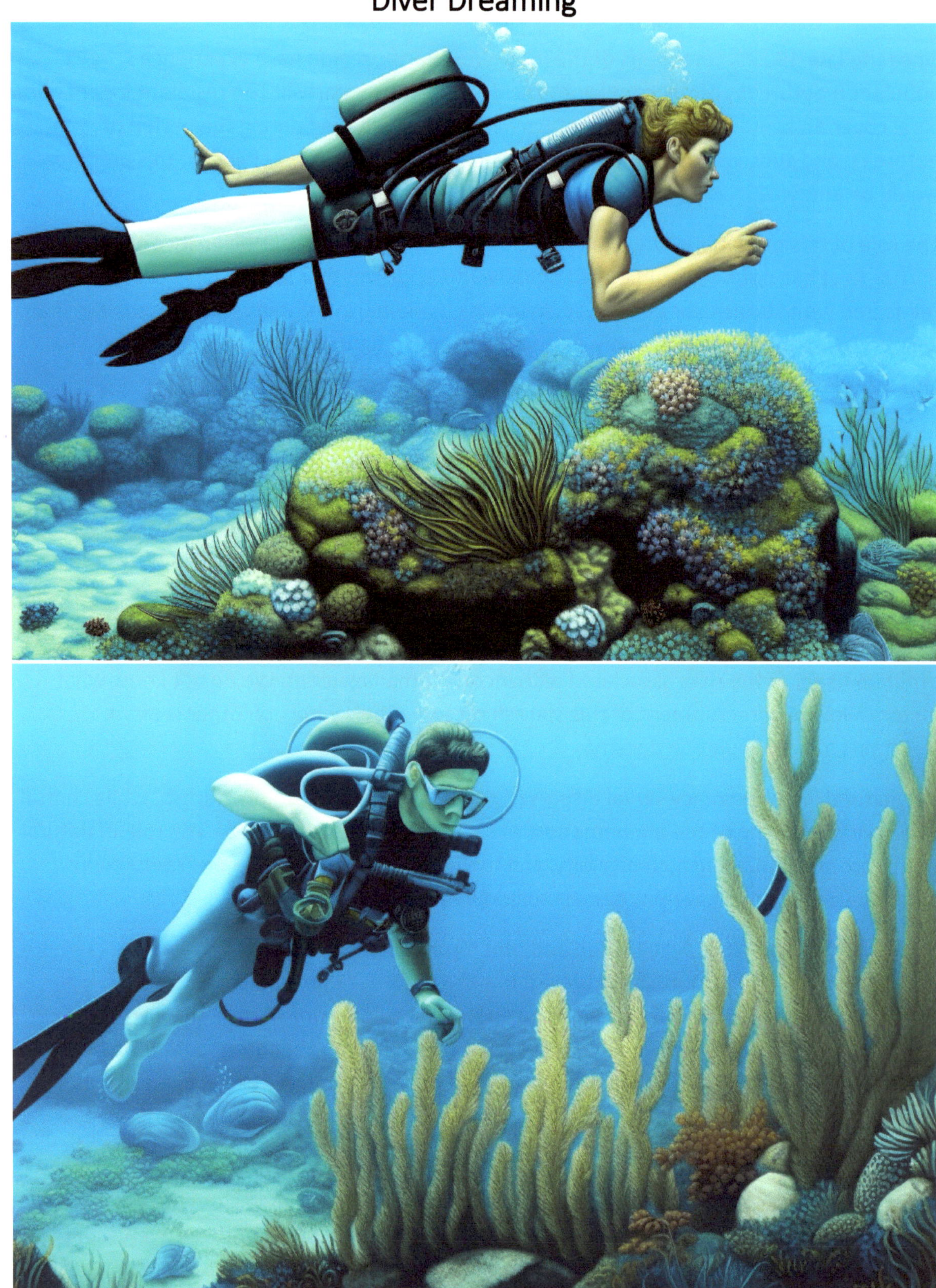

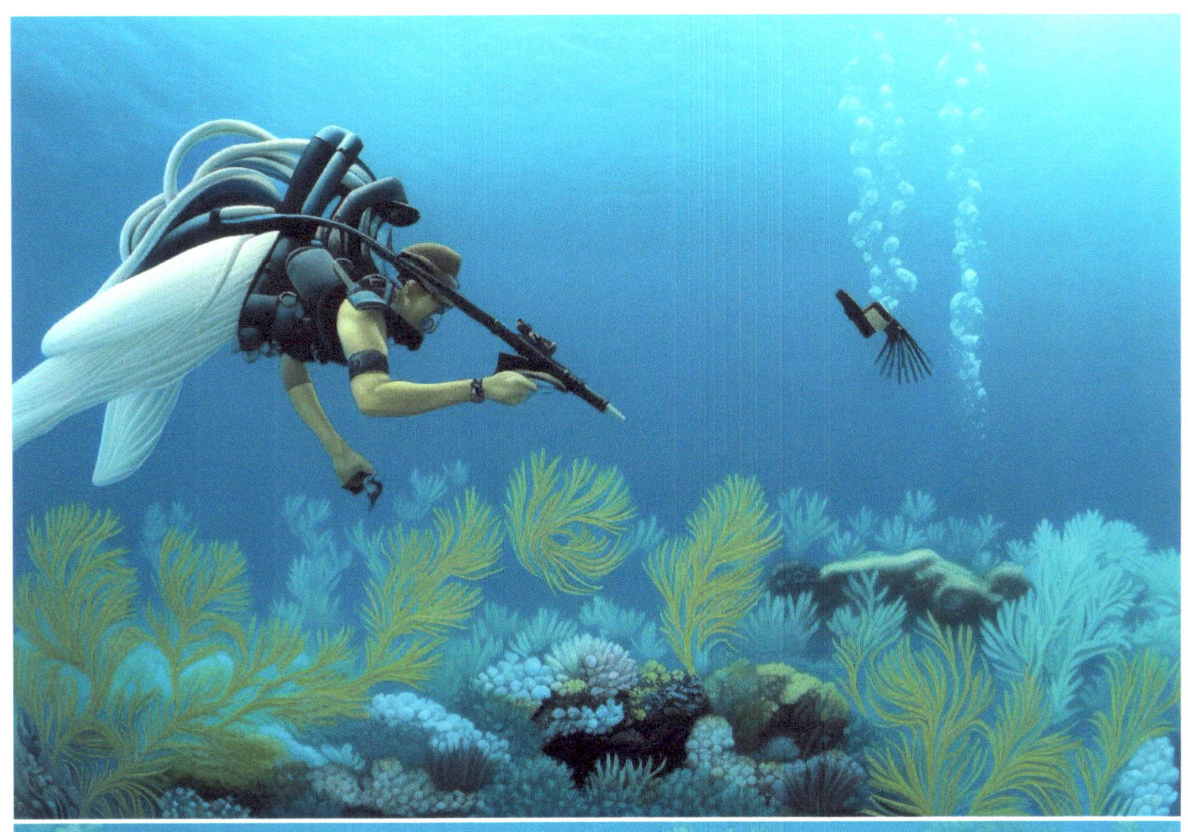

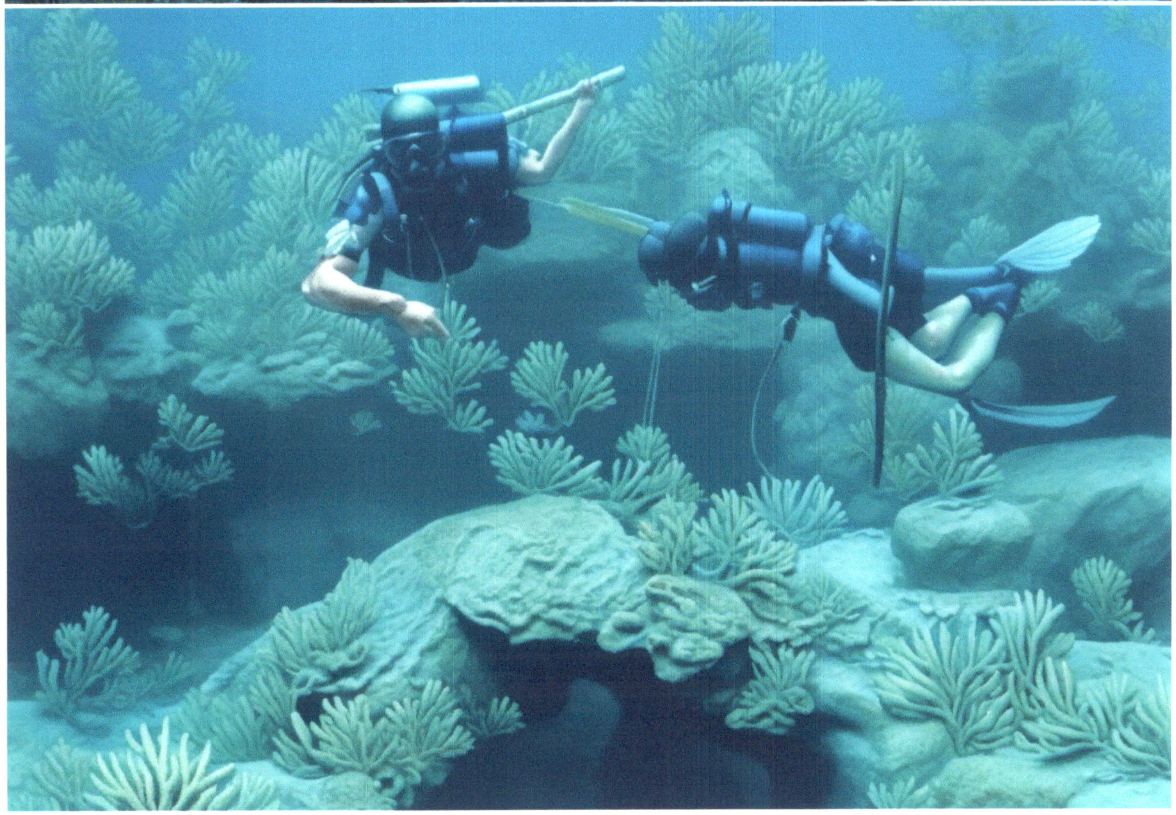

Algae Dreaming

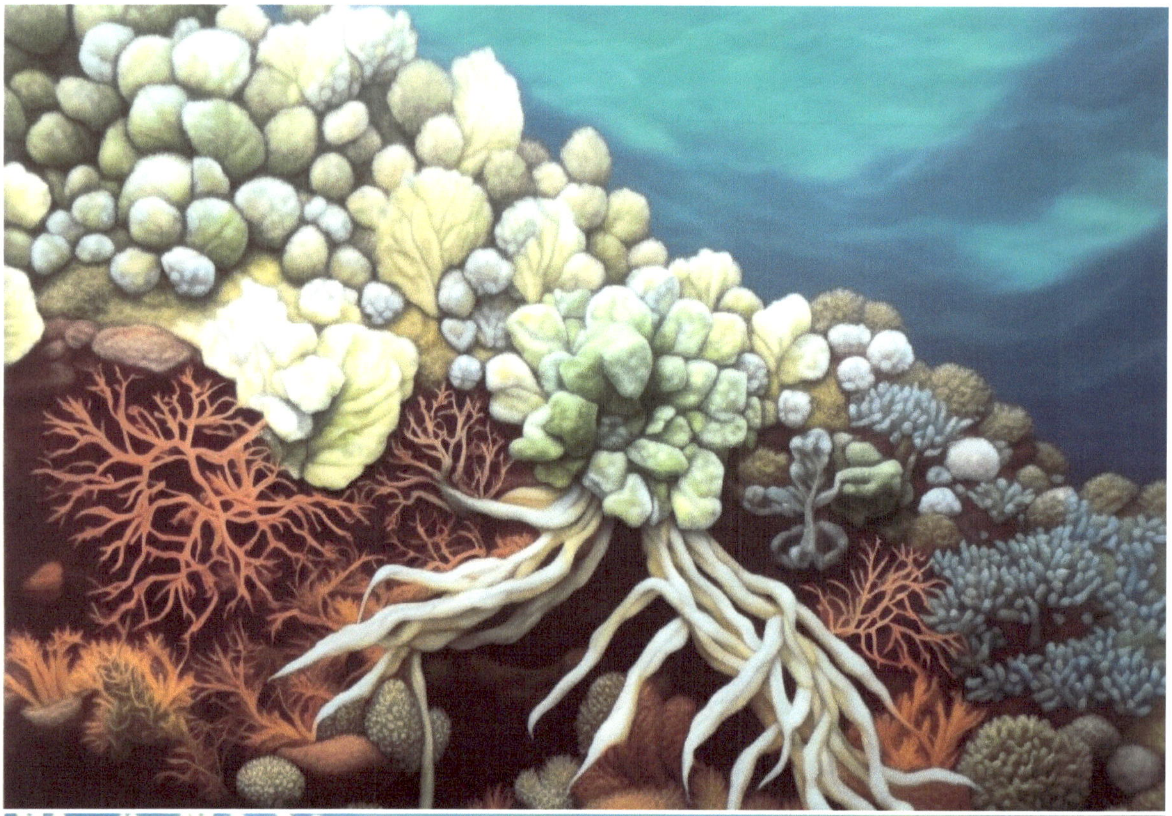

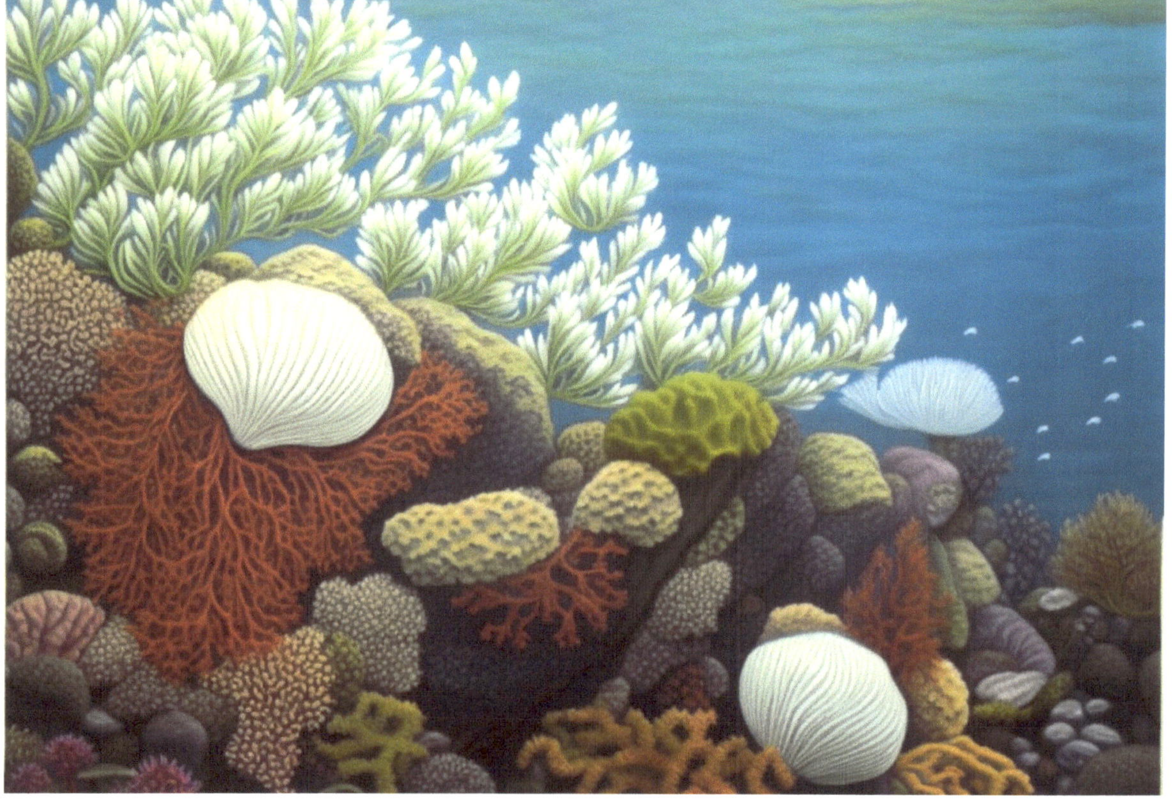

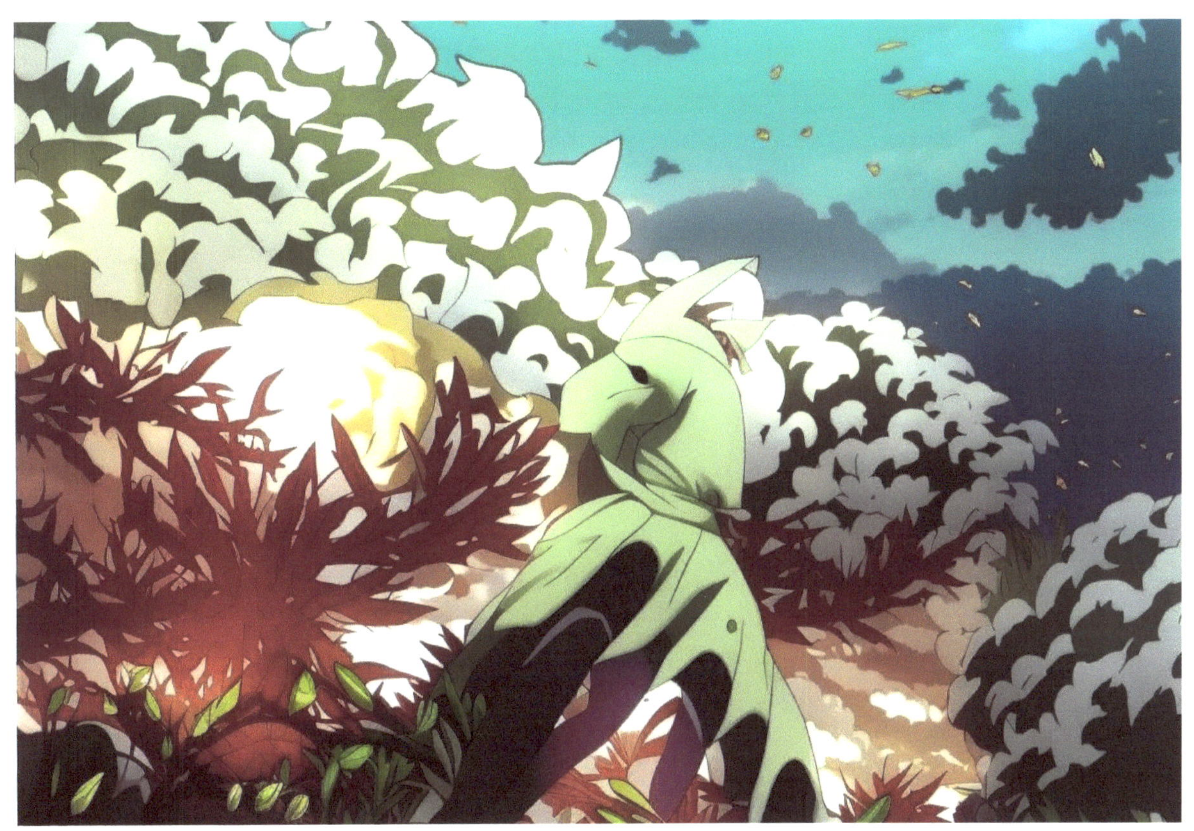

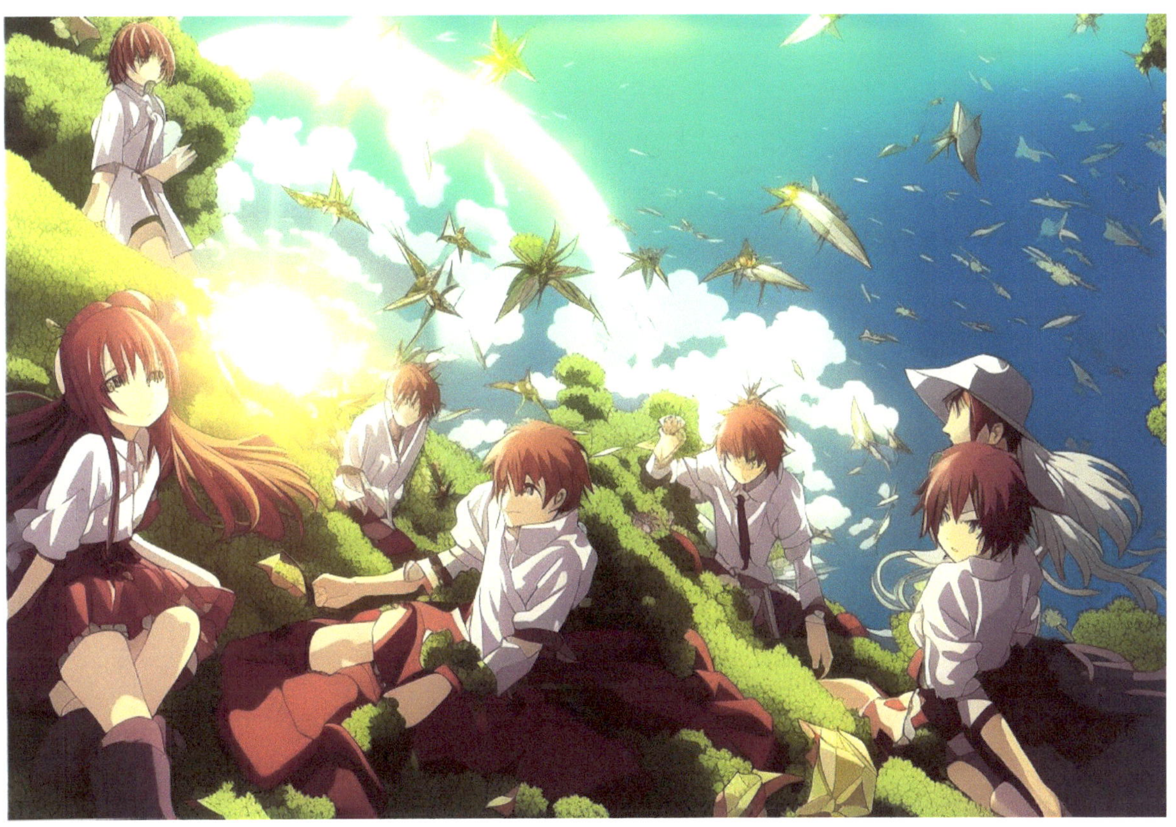

Nudibranch Dreaming

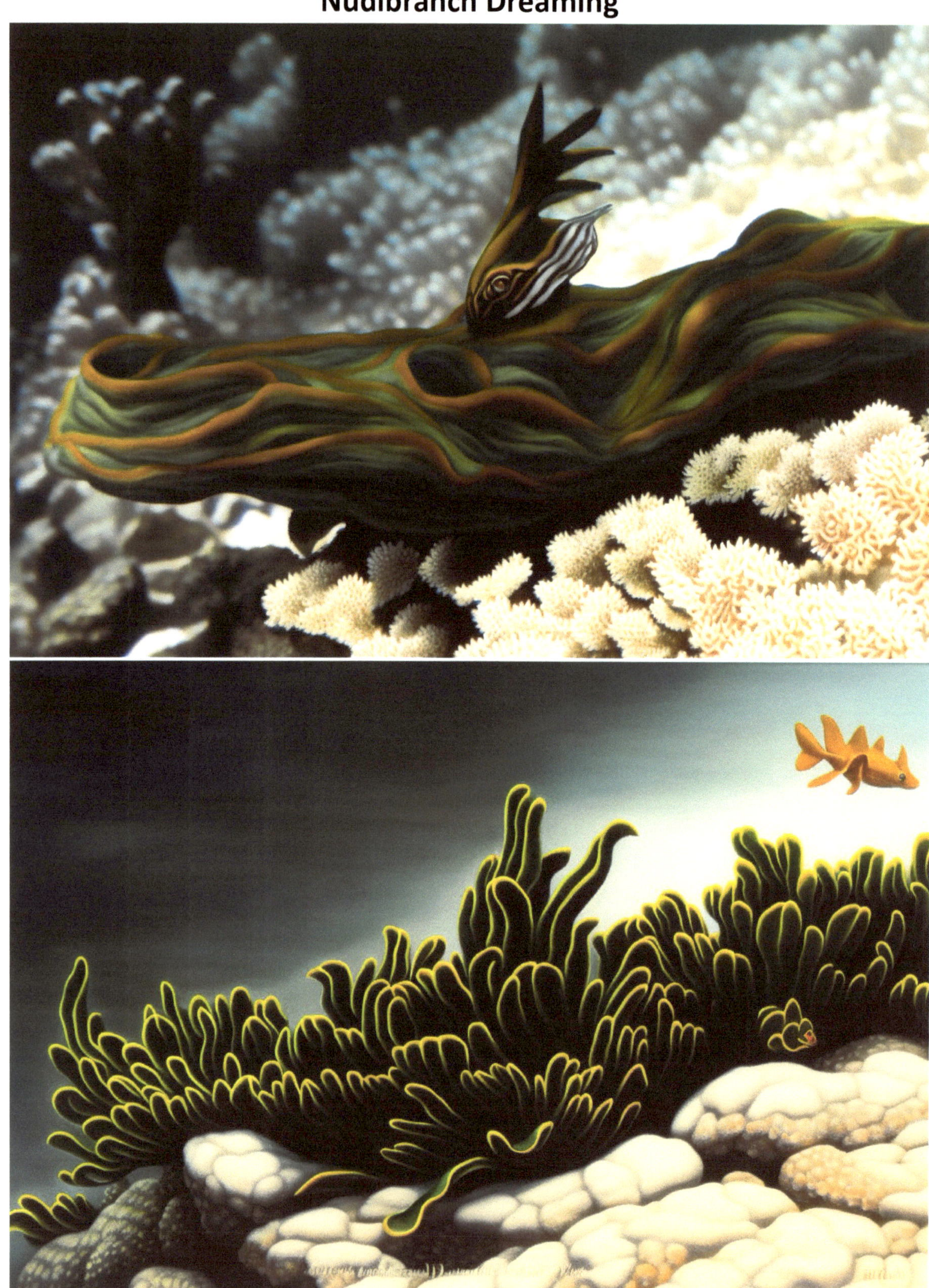

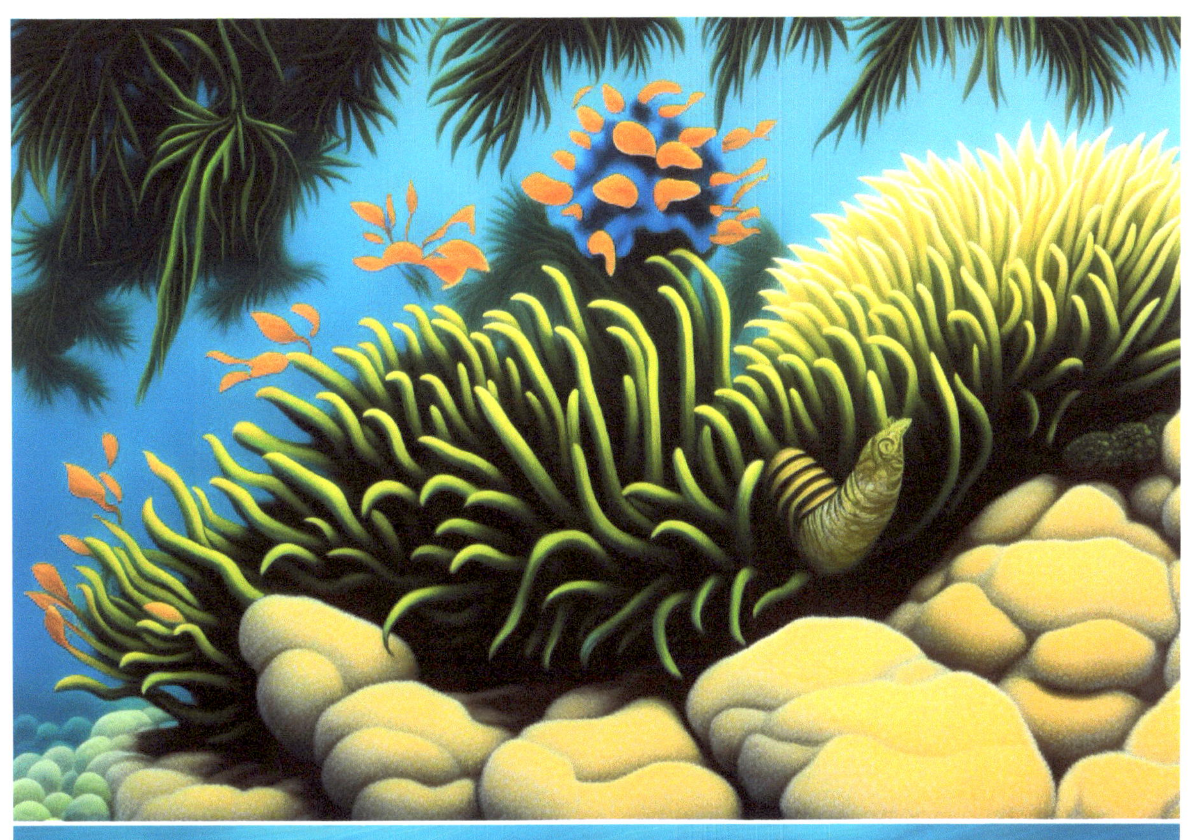

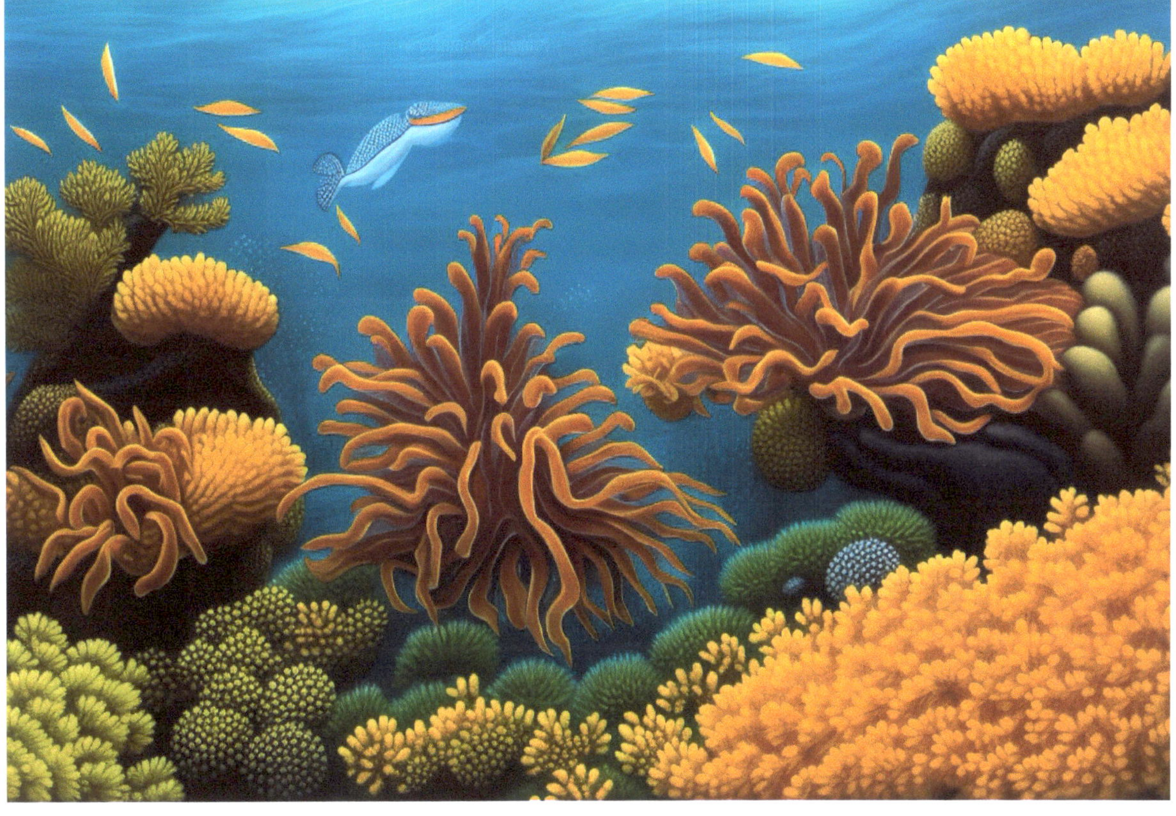

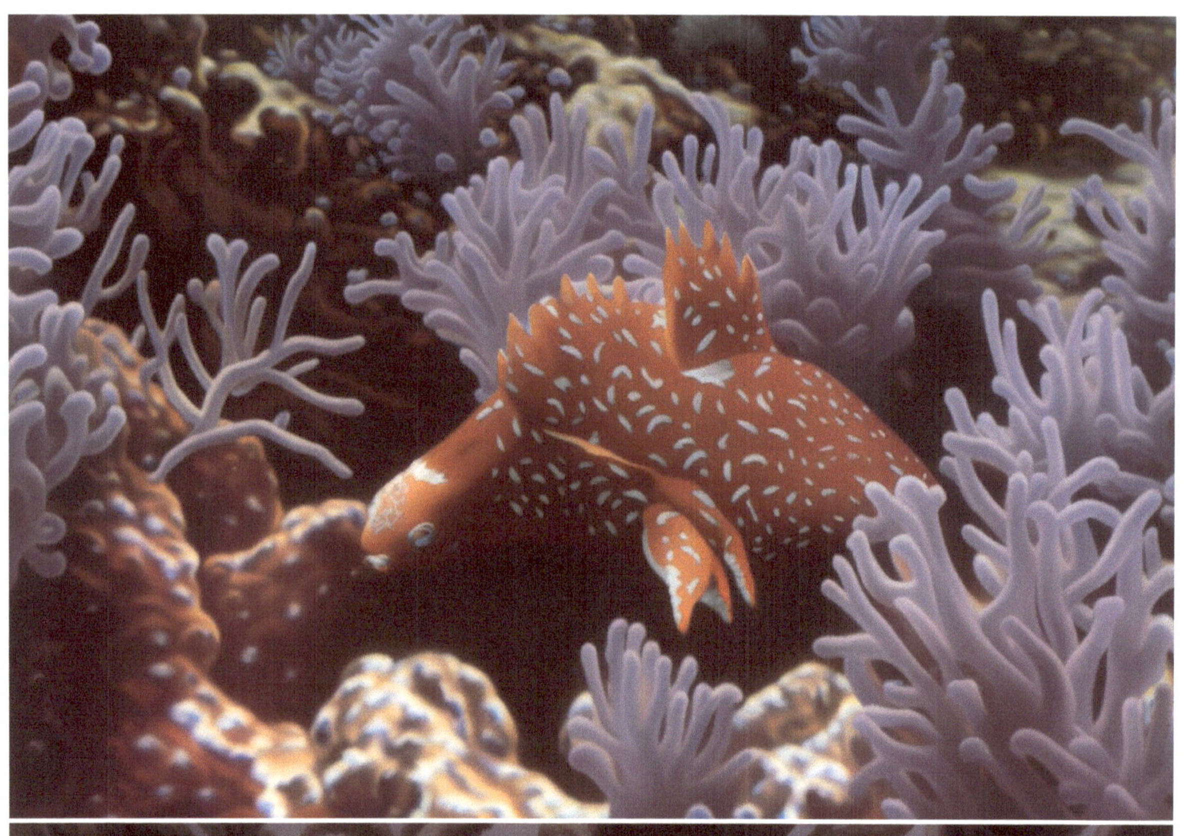

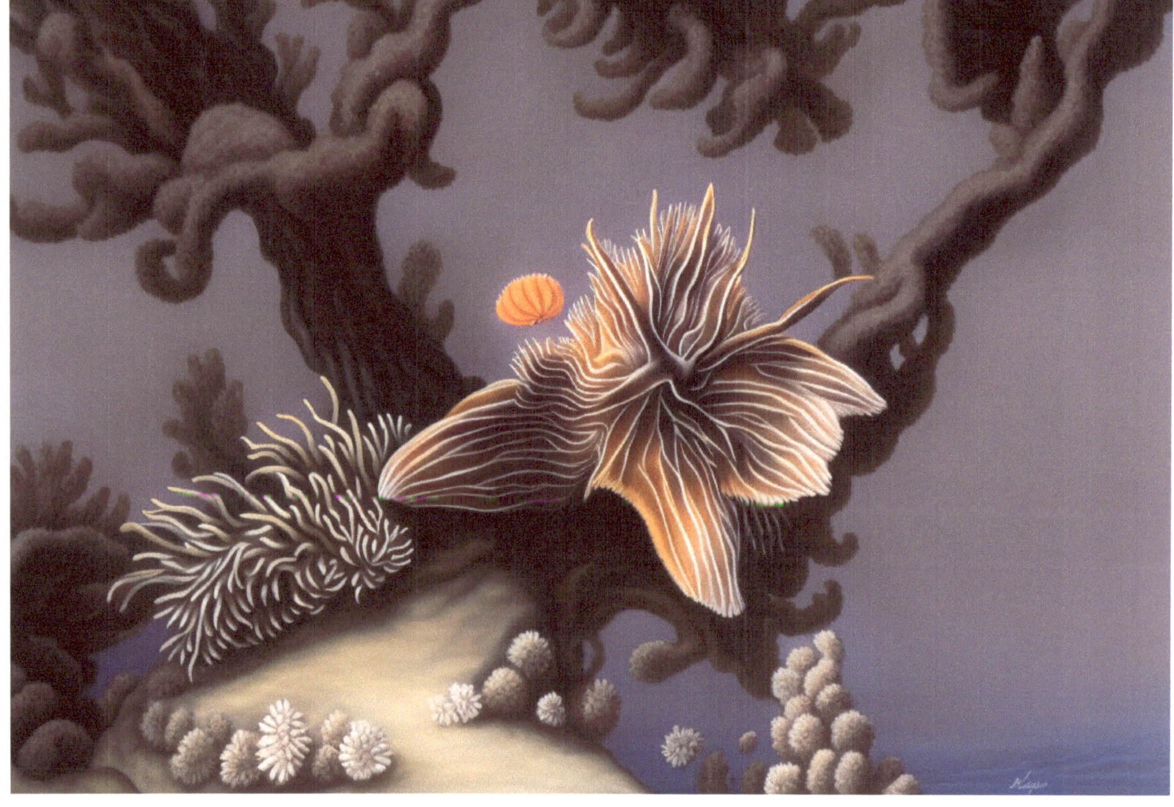

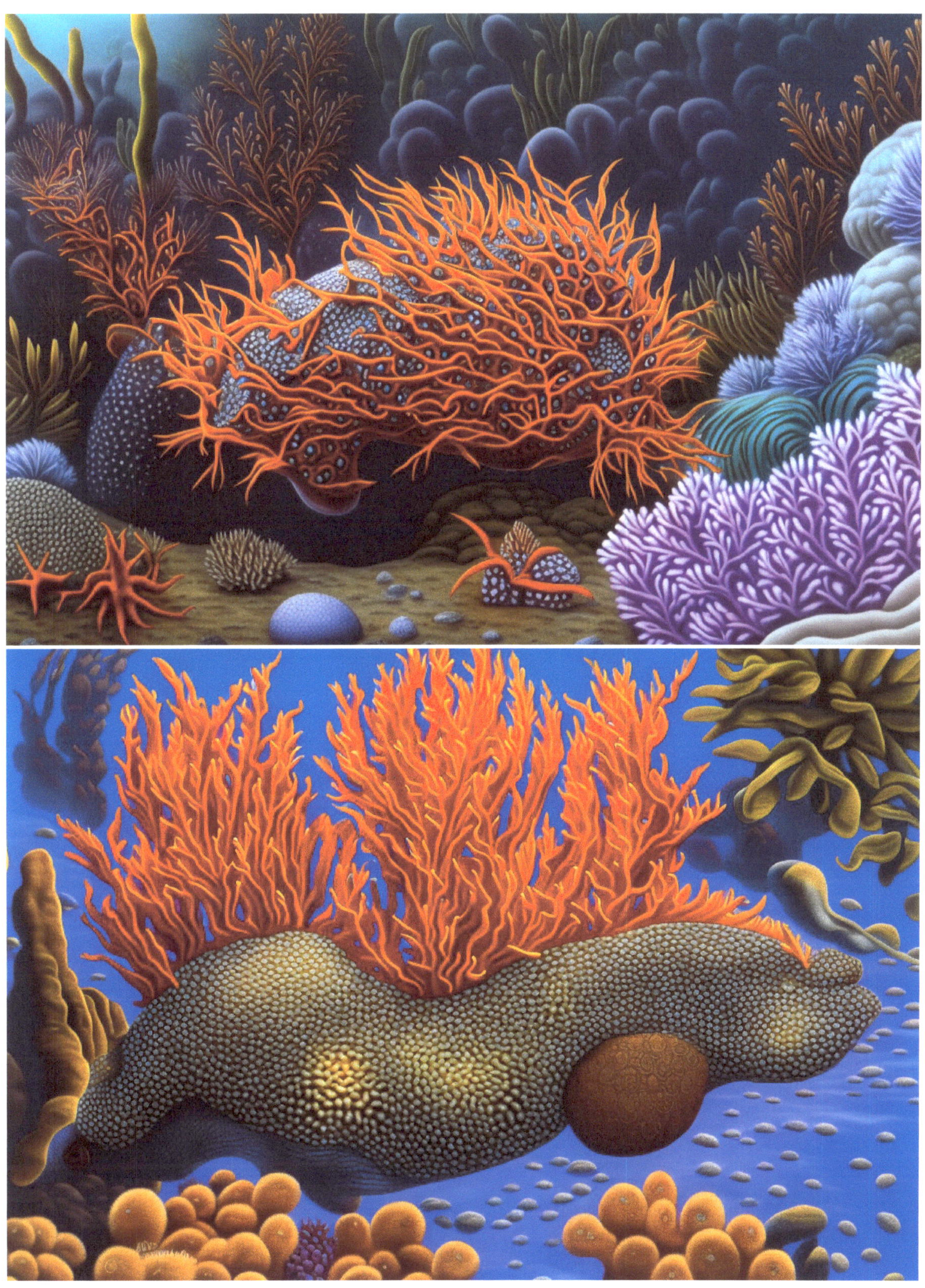

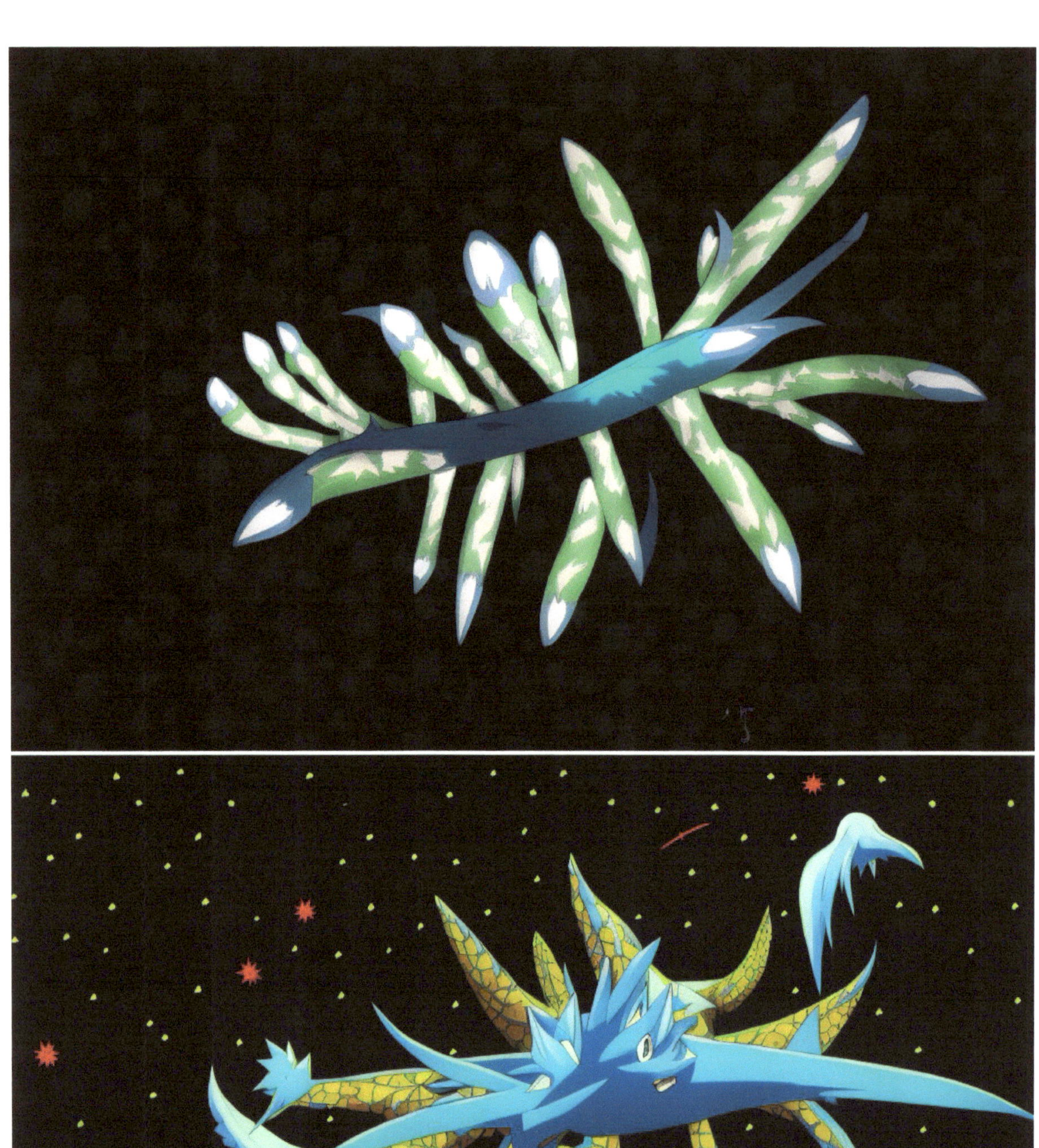

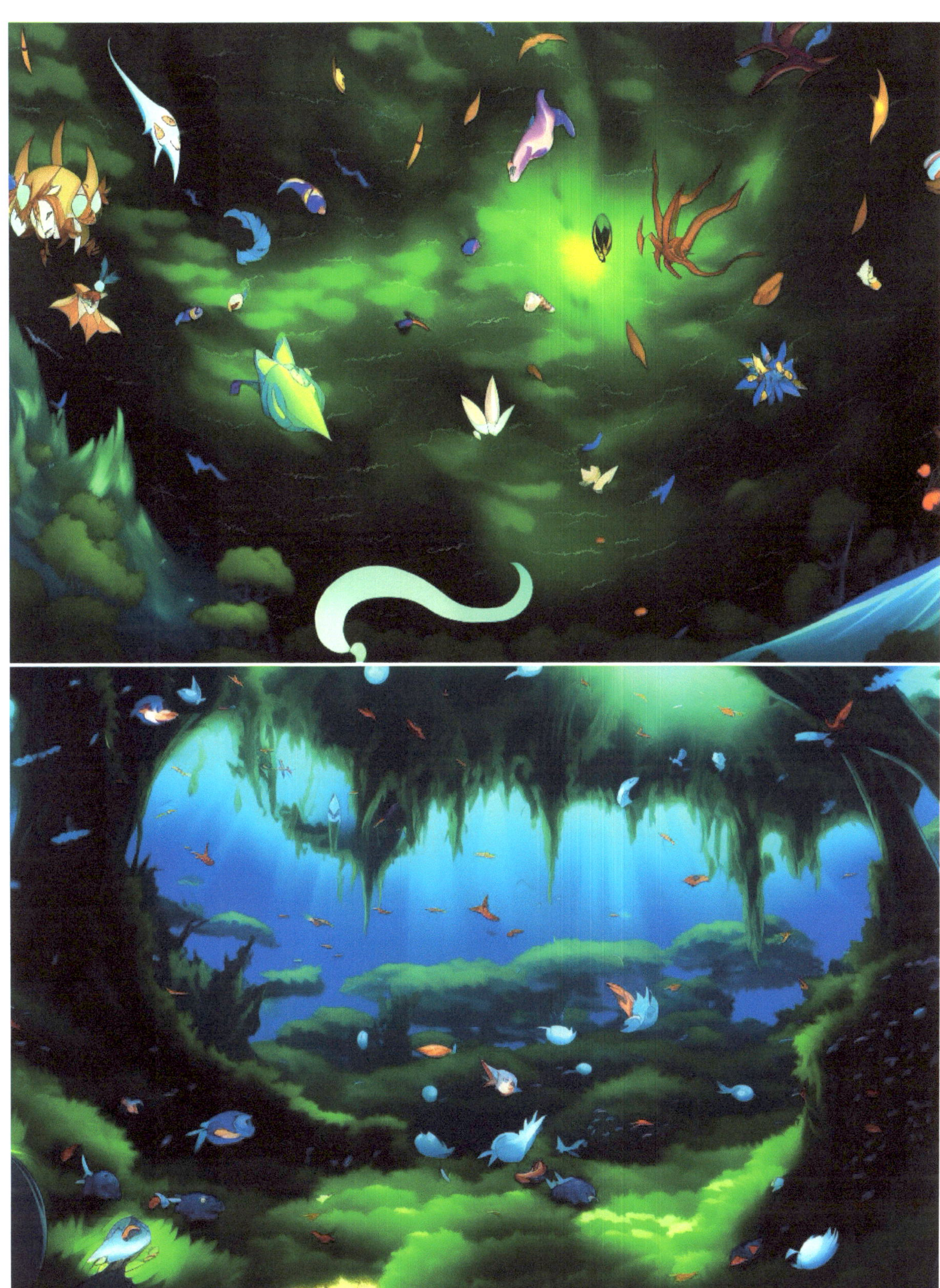

Sponge Dreaming

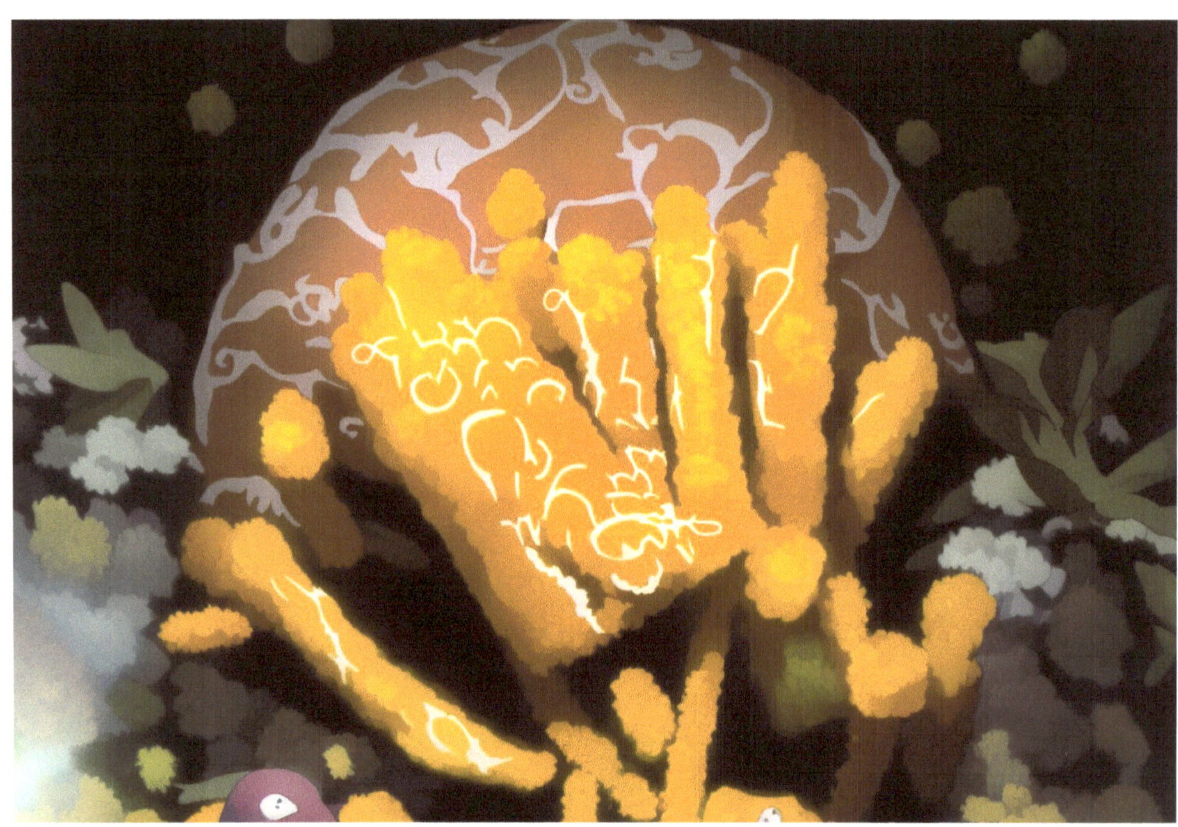

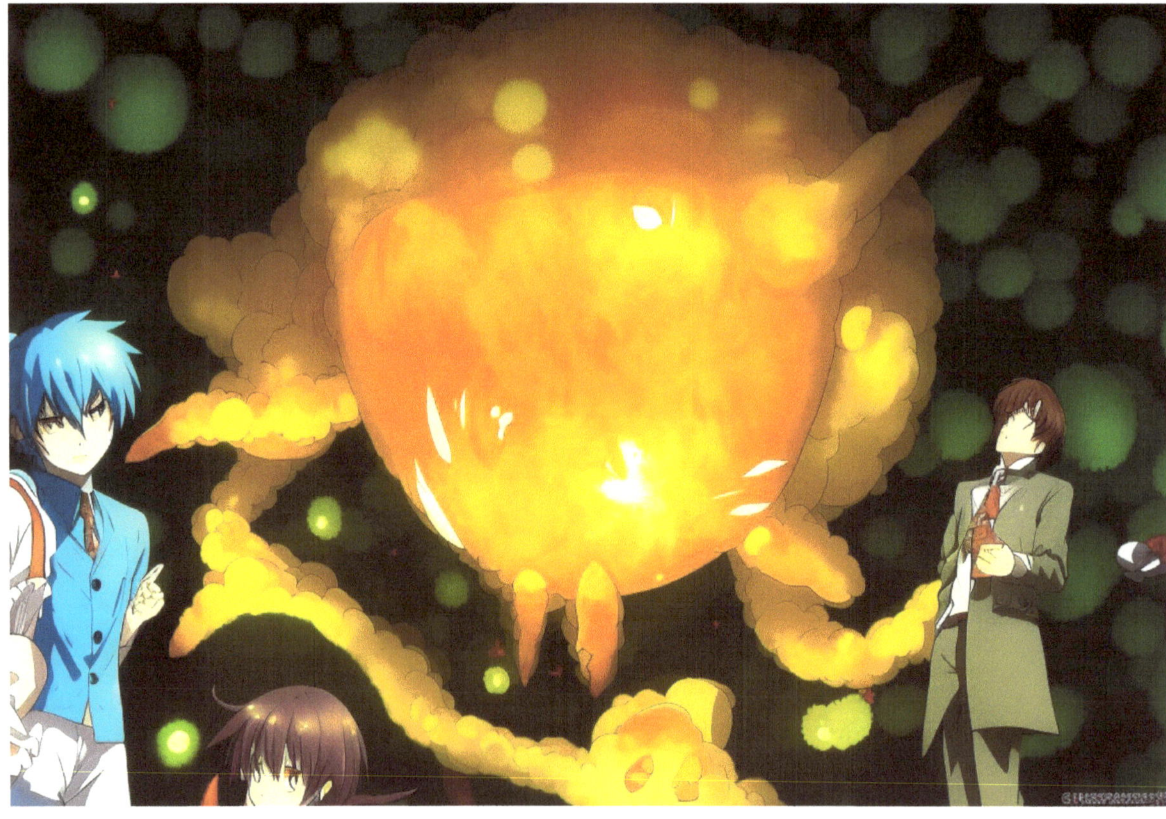

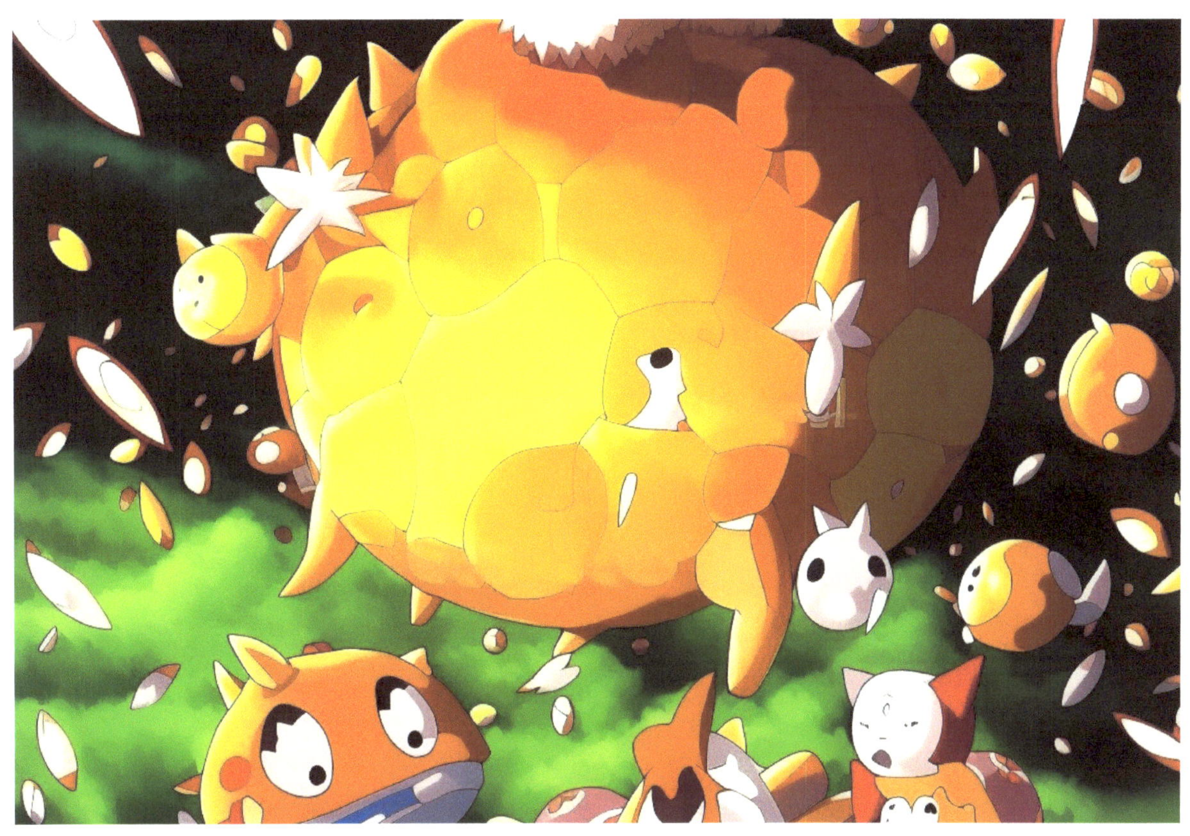

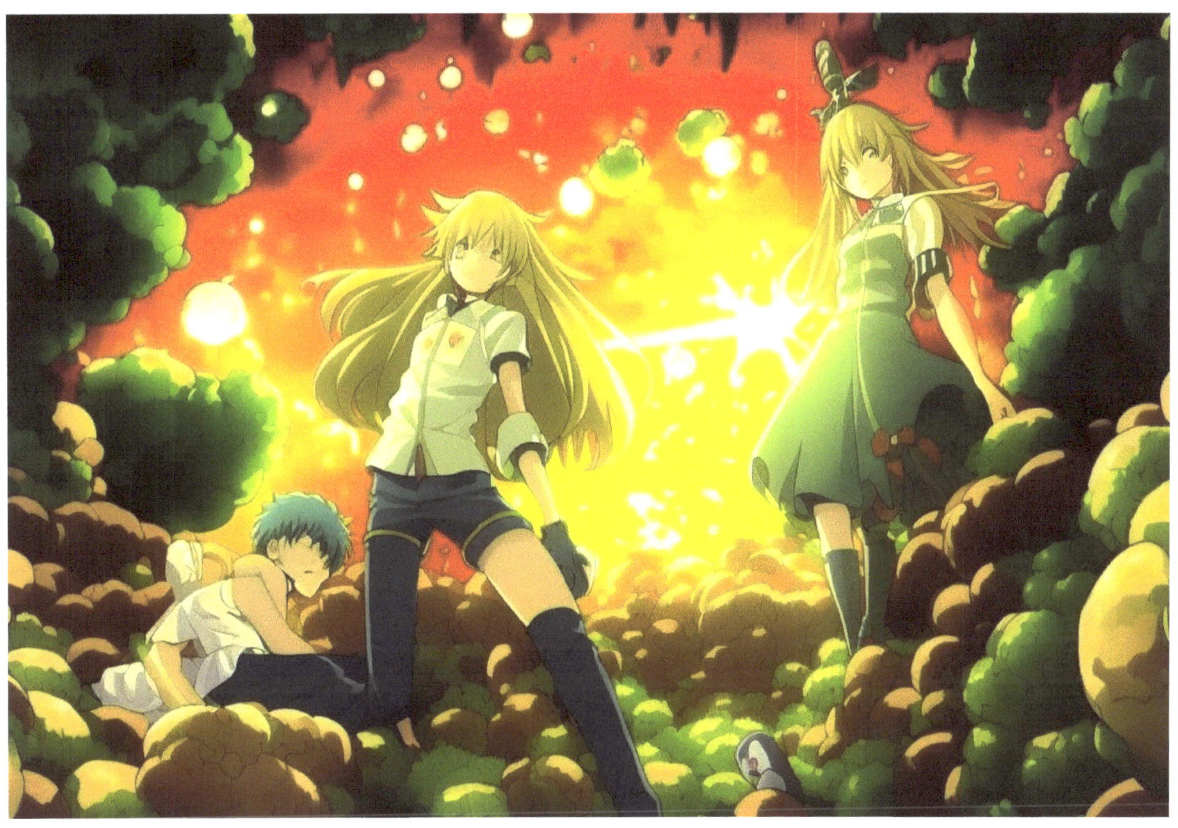

Protula Dreaming

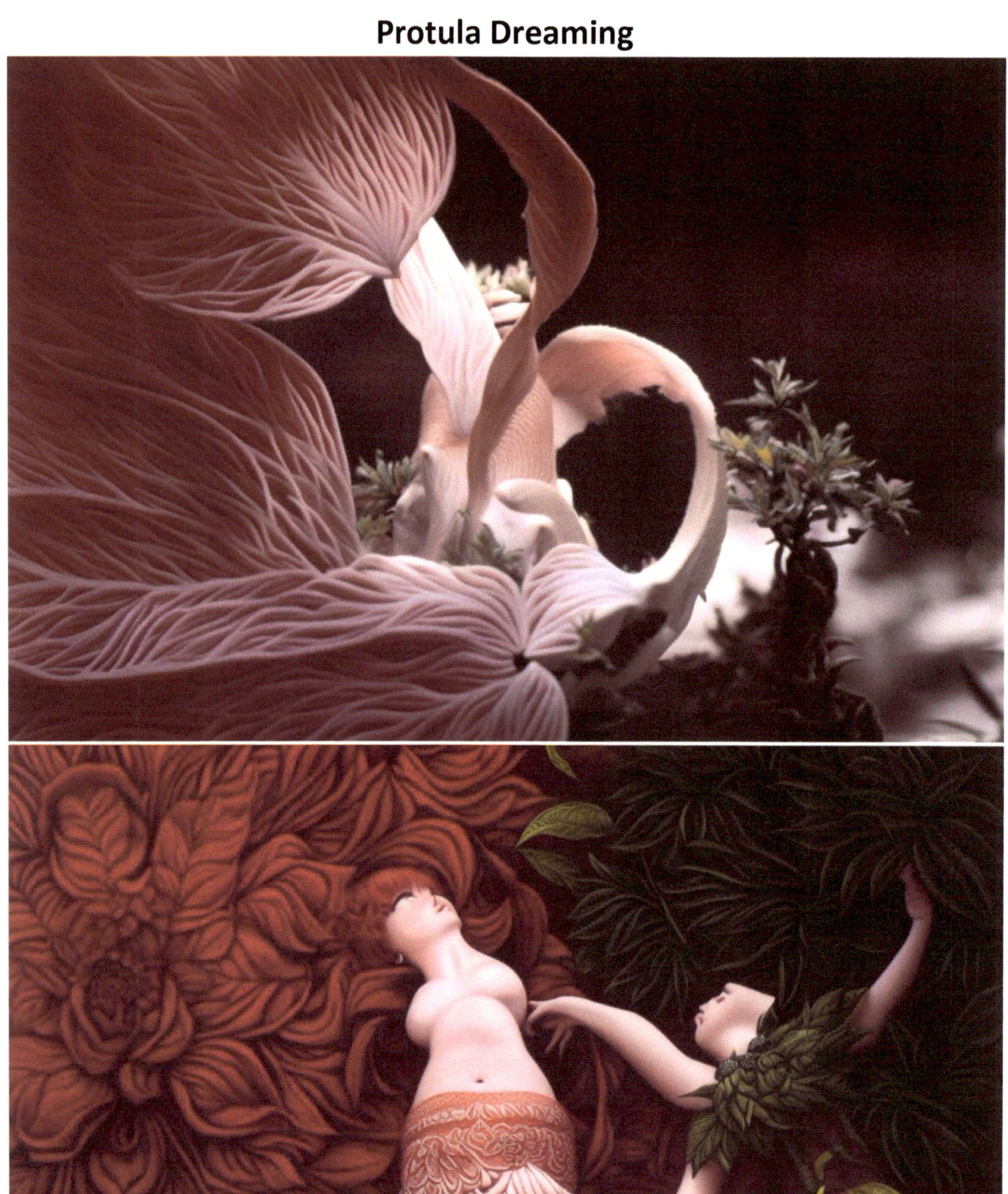

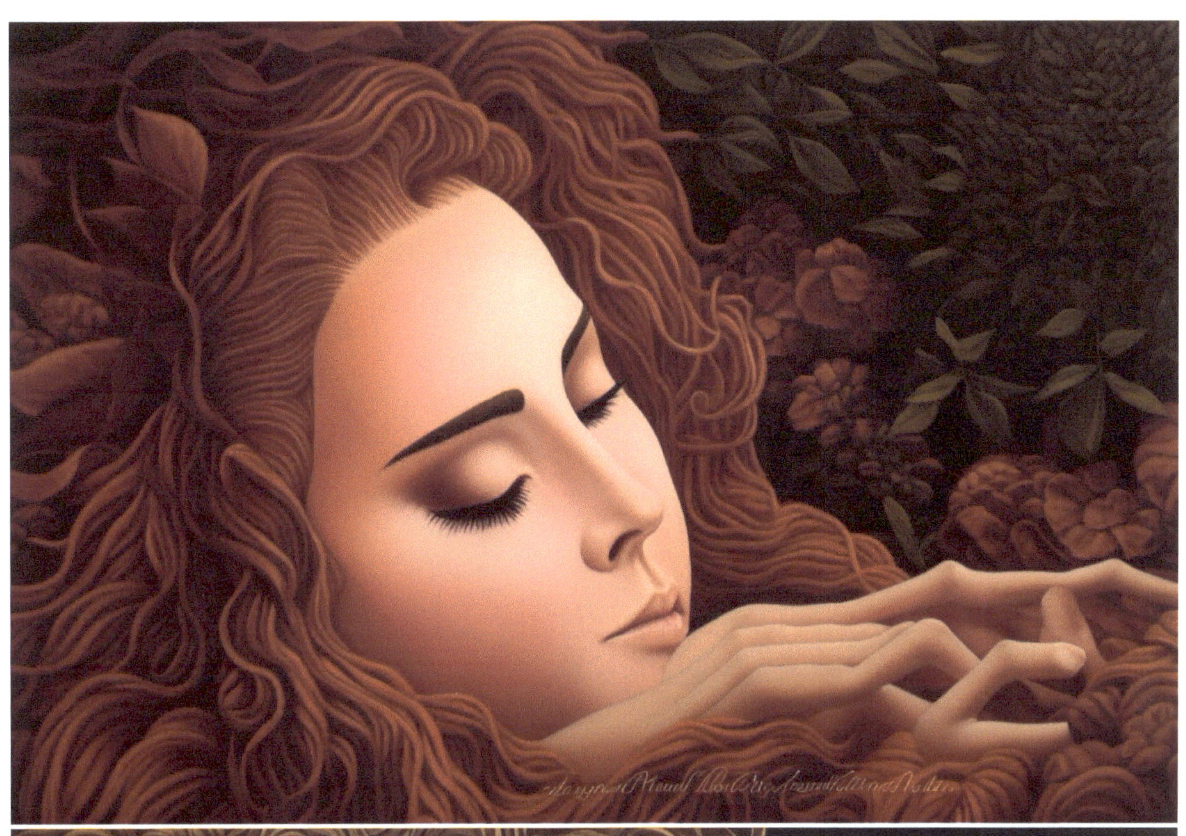

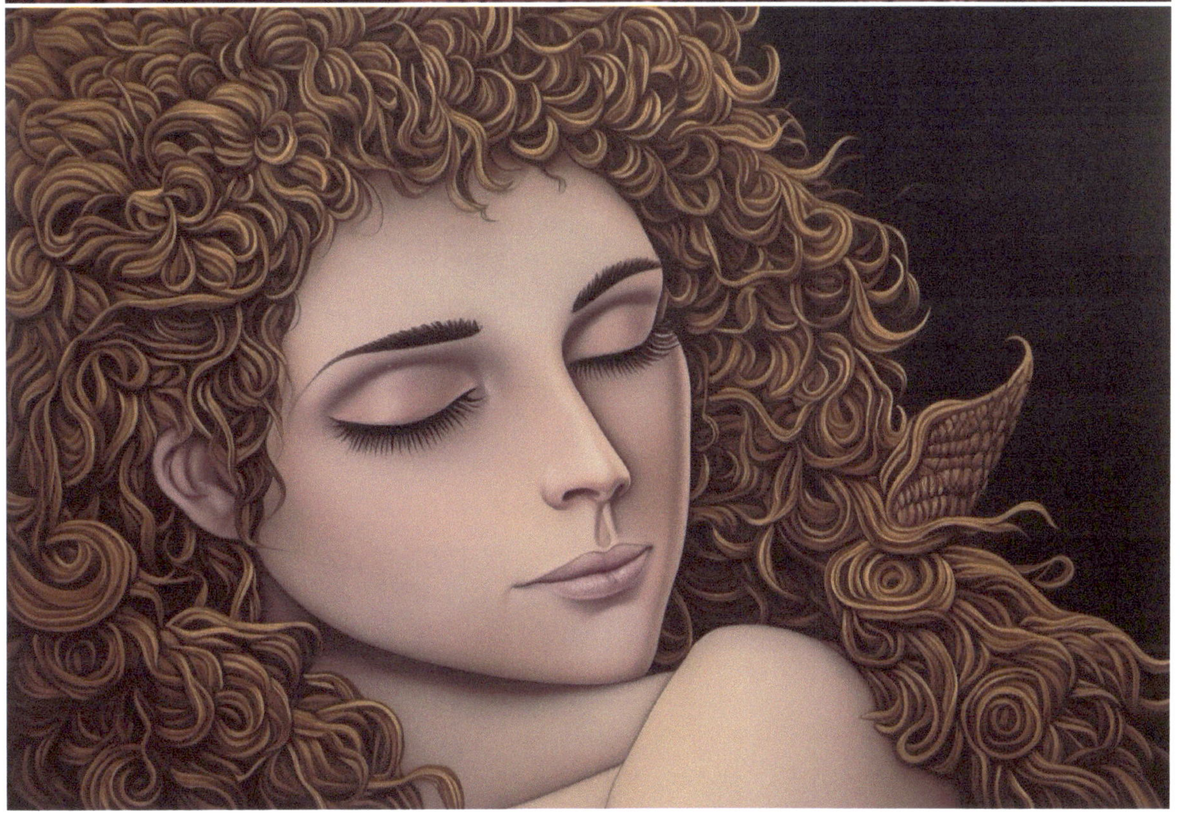

Clam Dreaming

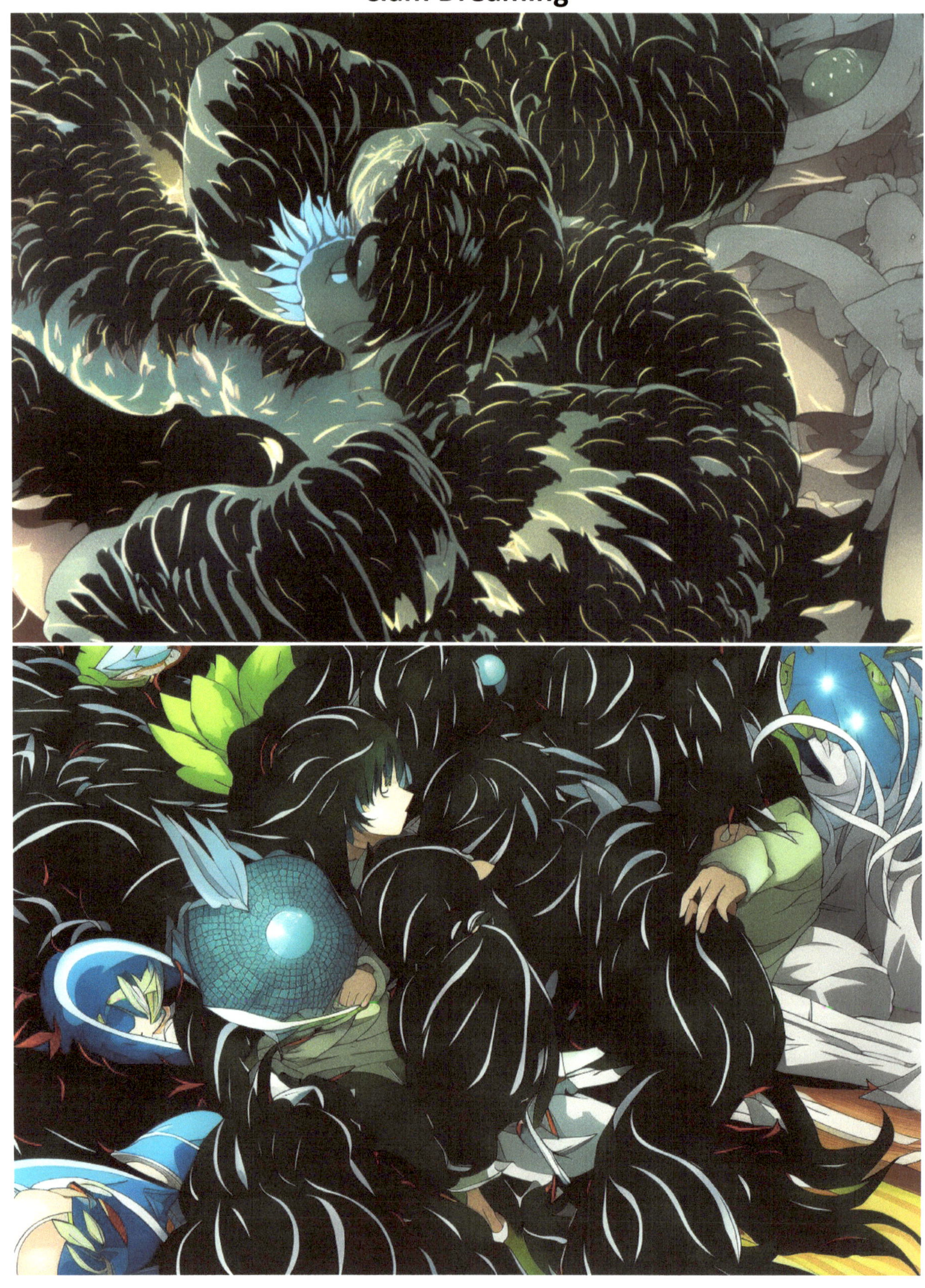

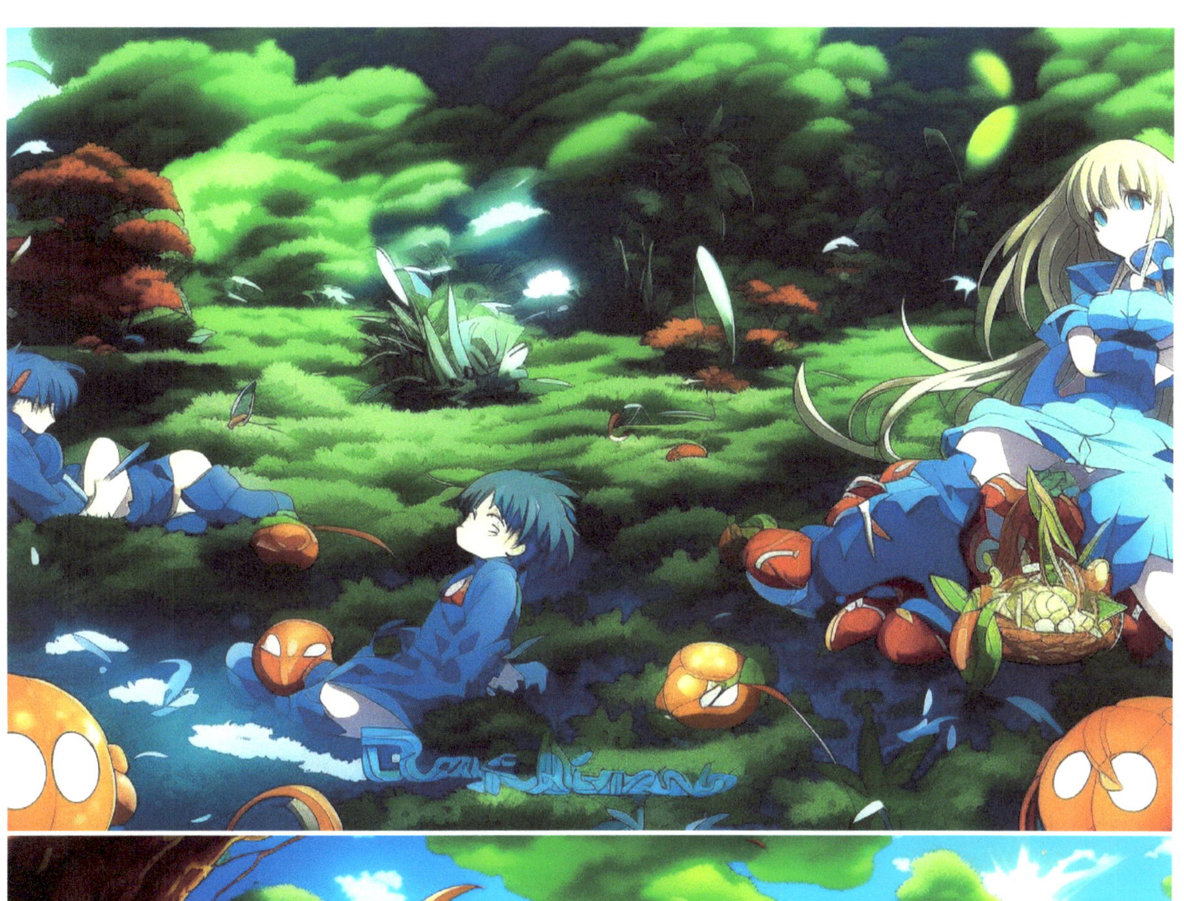

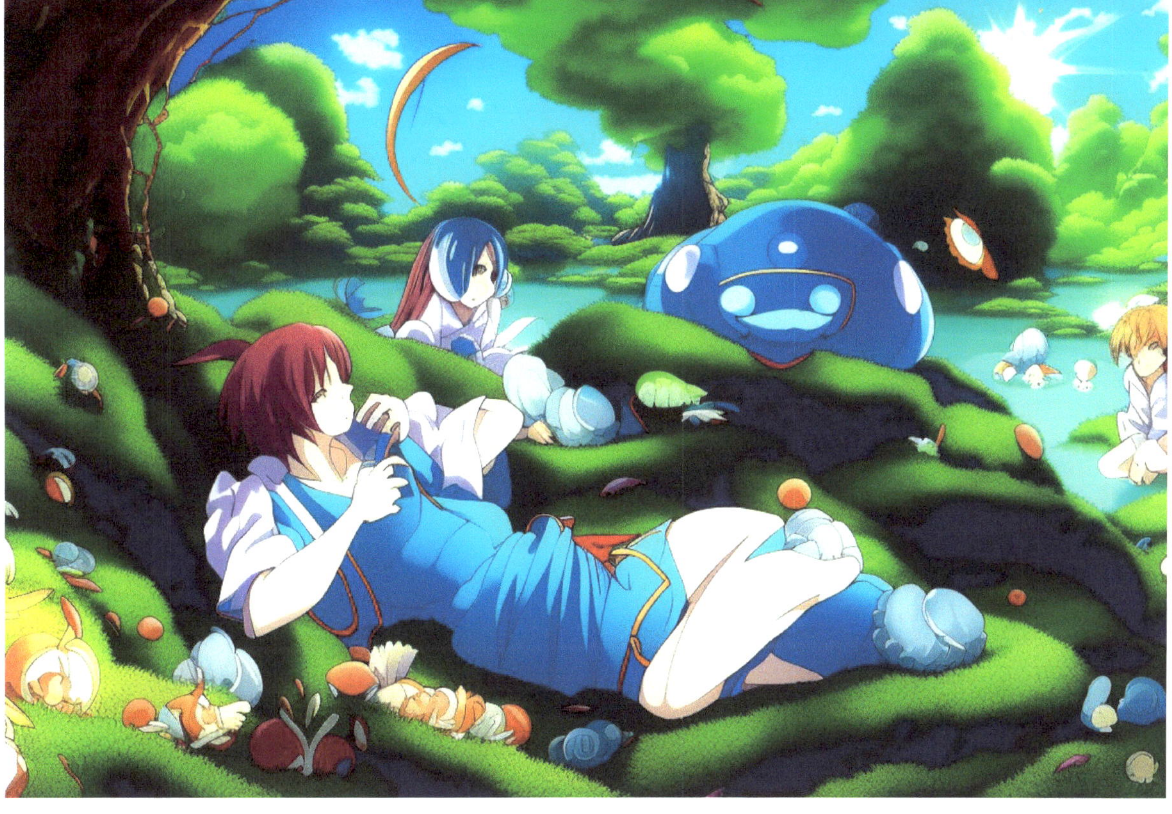

Ascidian Dreaming

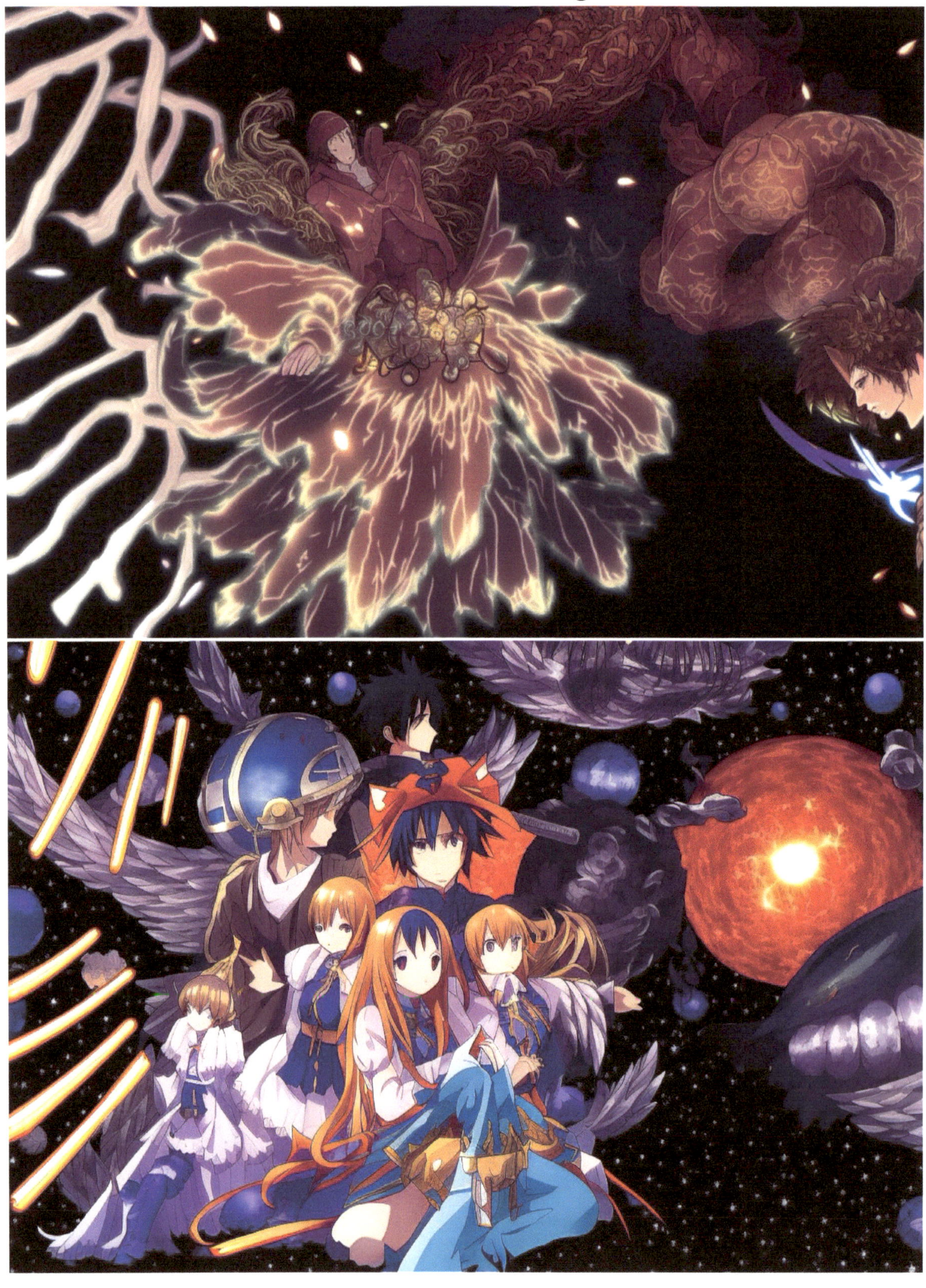

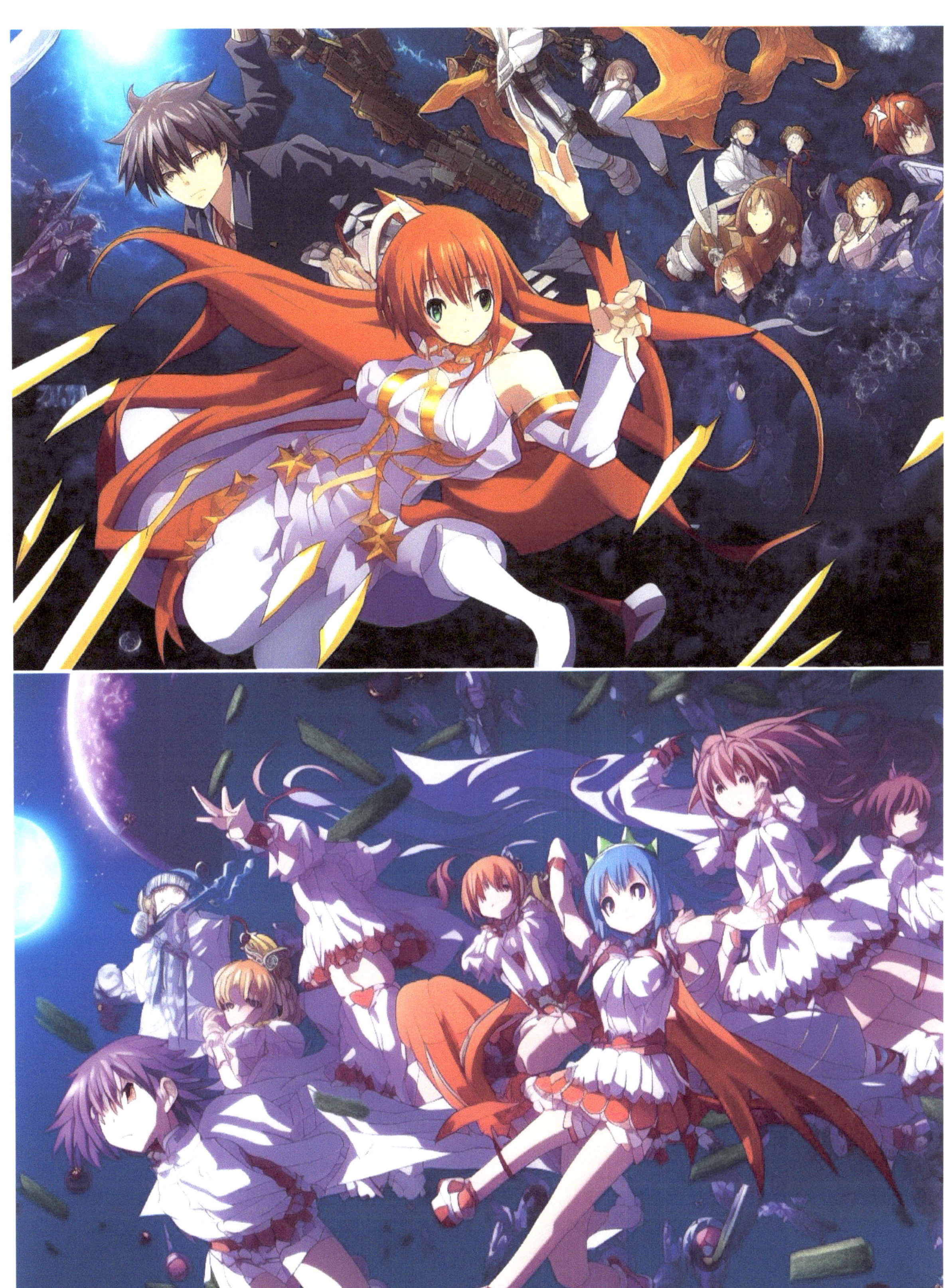

Blue Angelfish Dreaming

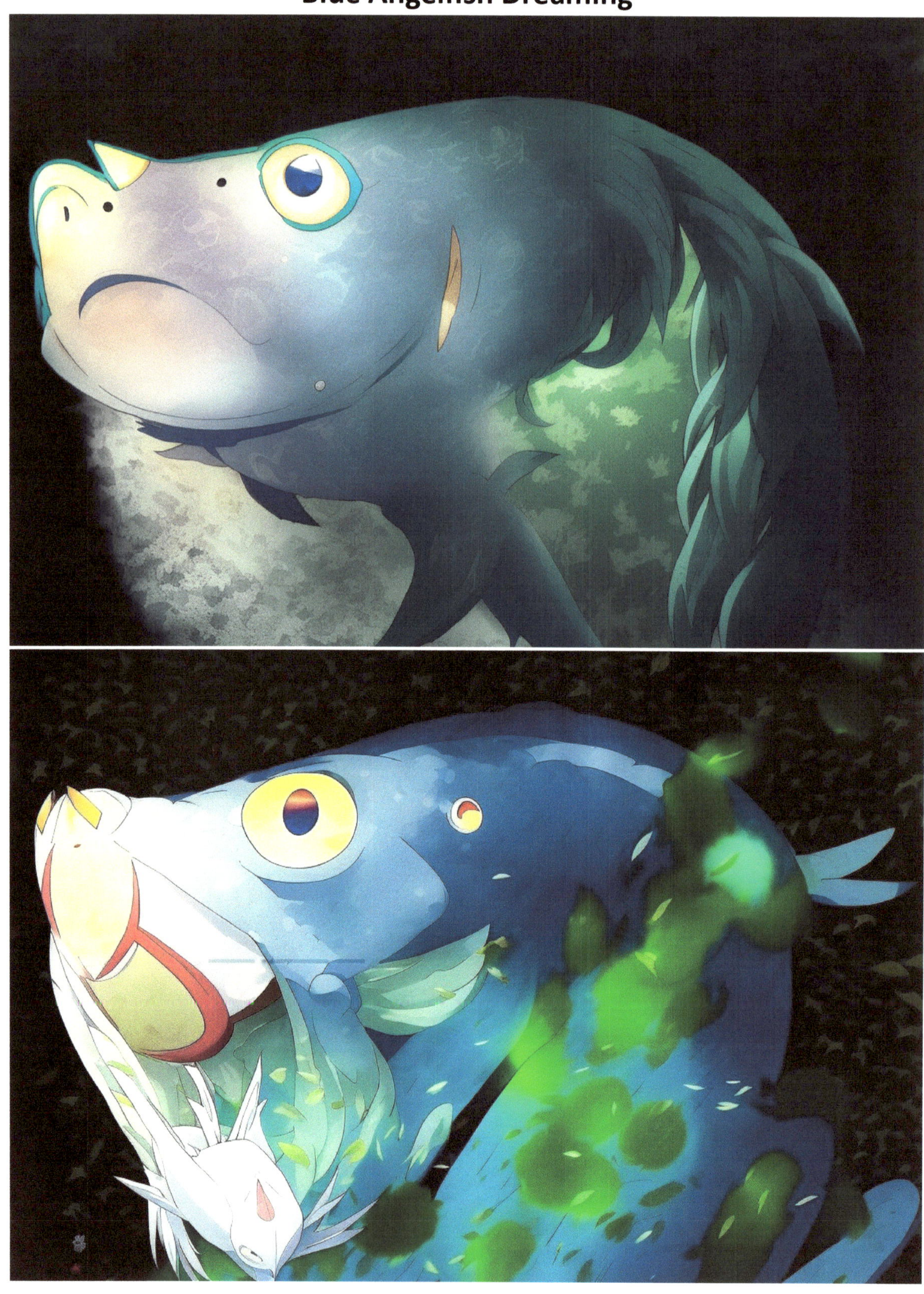

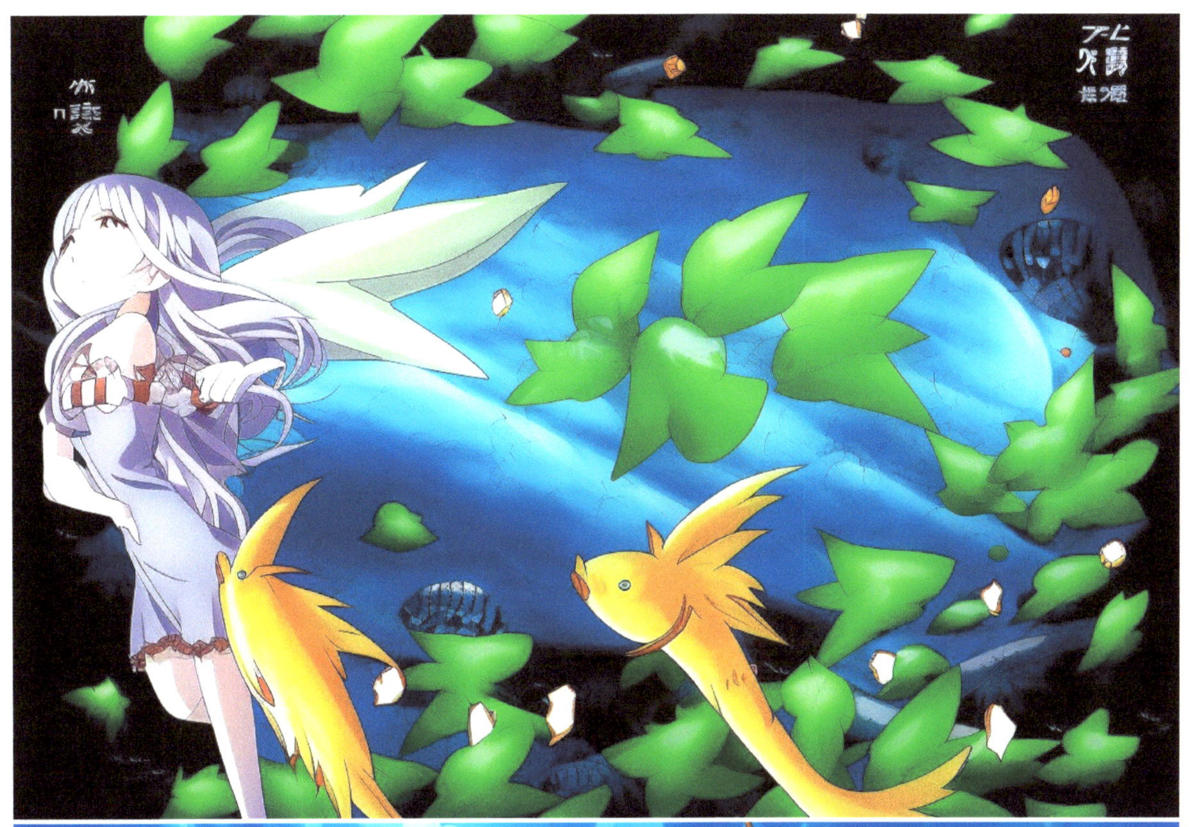

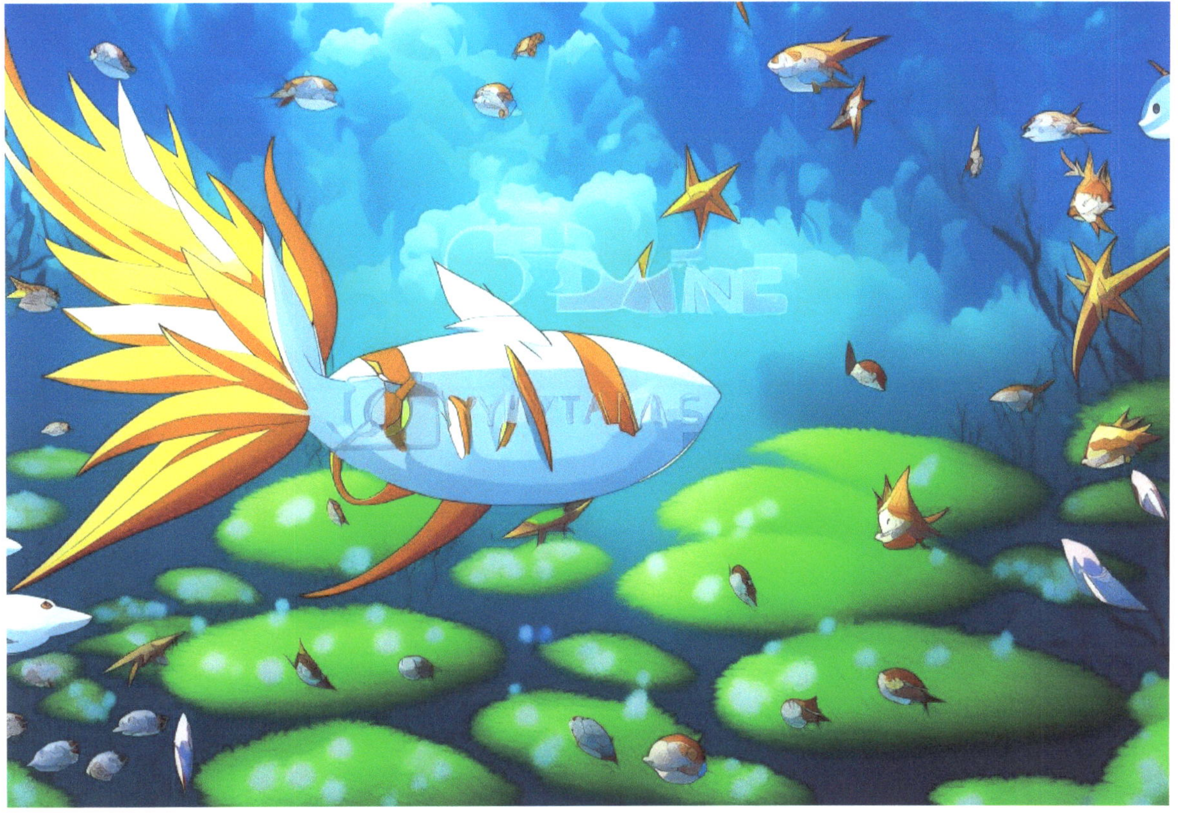

Coral Trout Dreaming

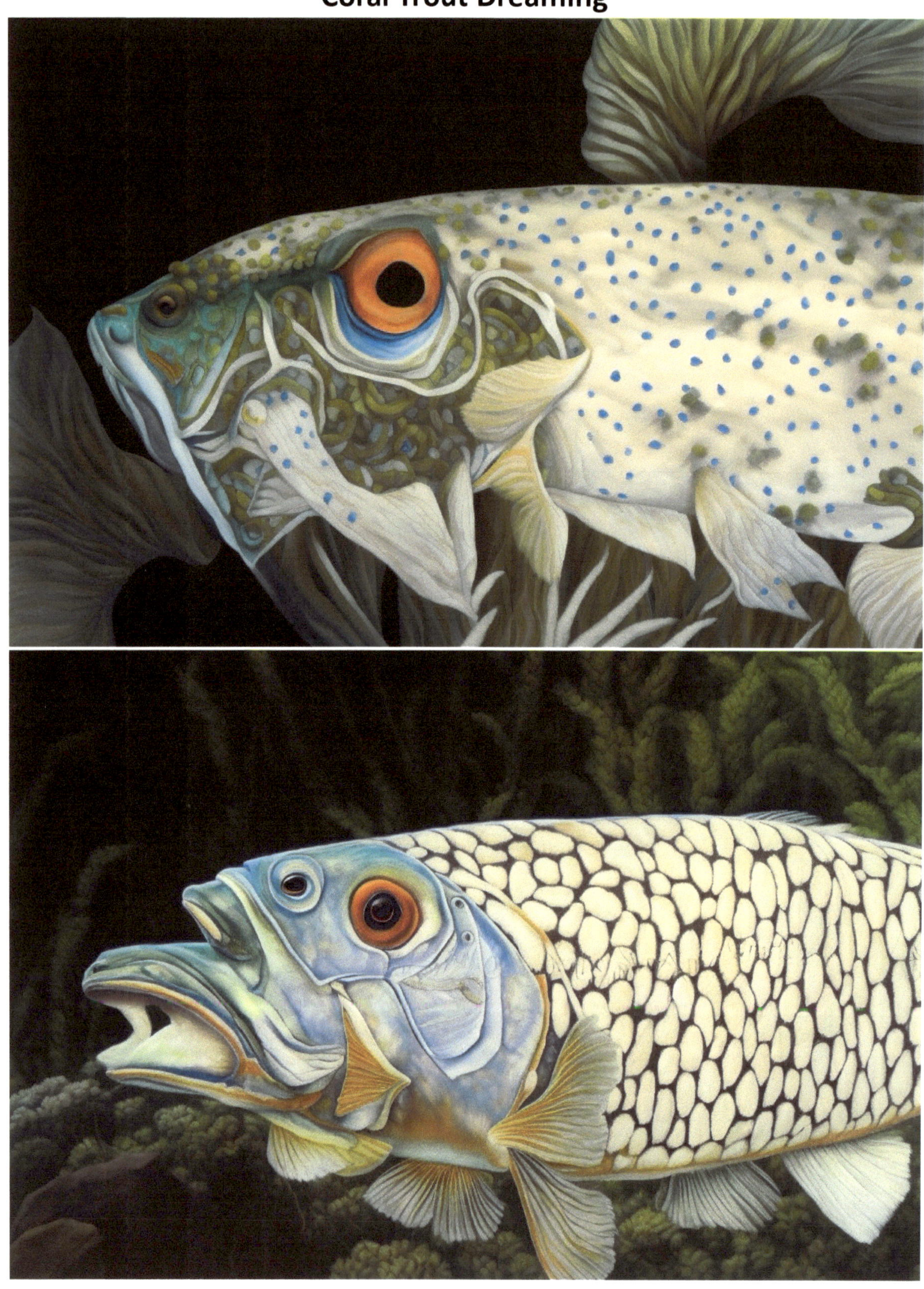

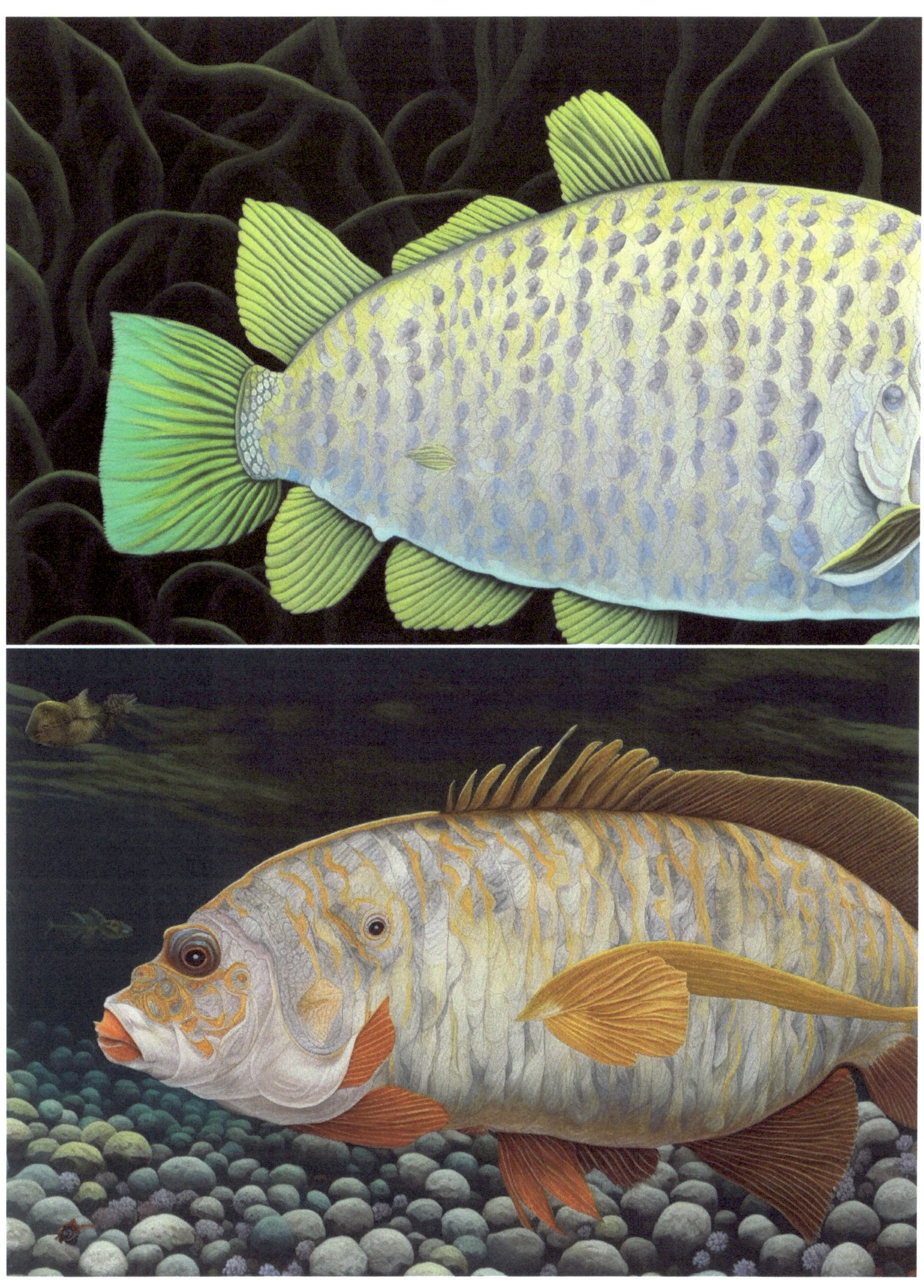

Rabbit Fish Dreaming

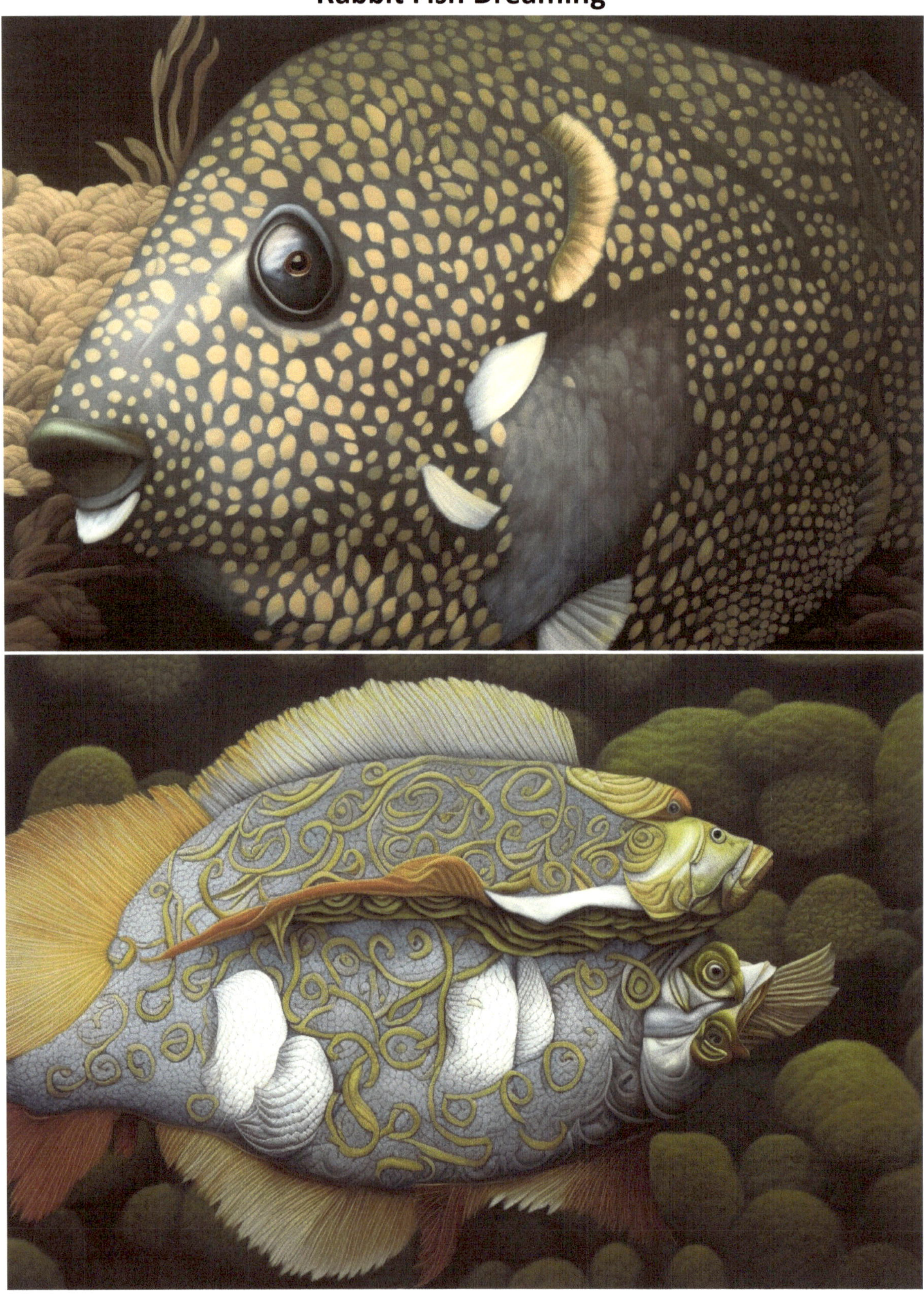

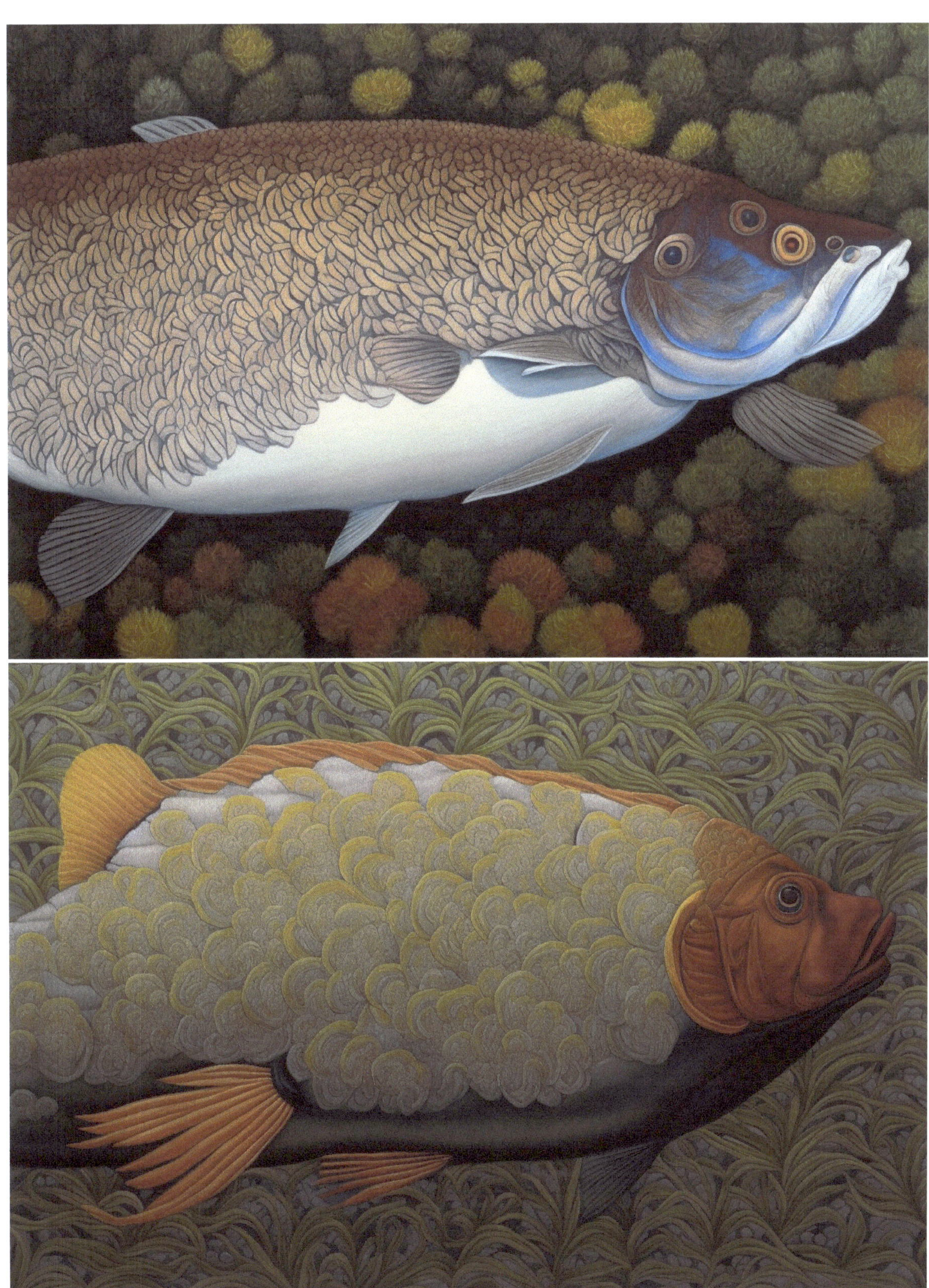

Soft Coral Dreaming

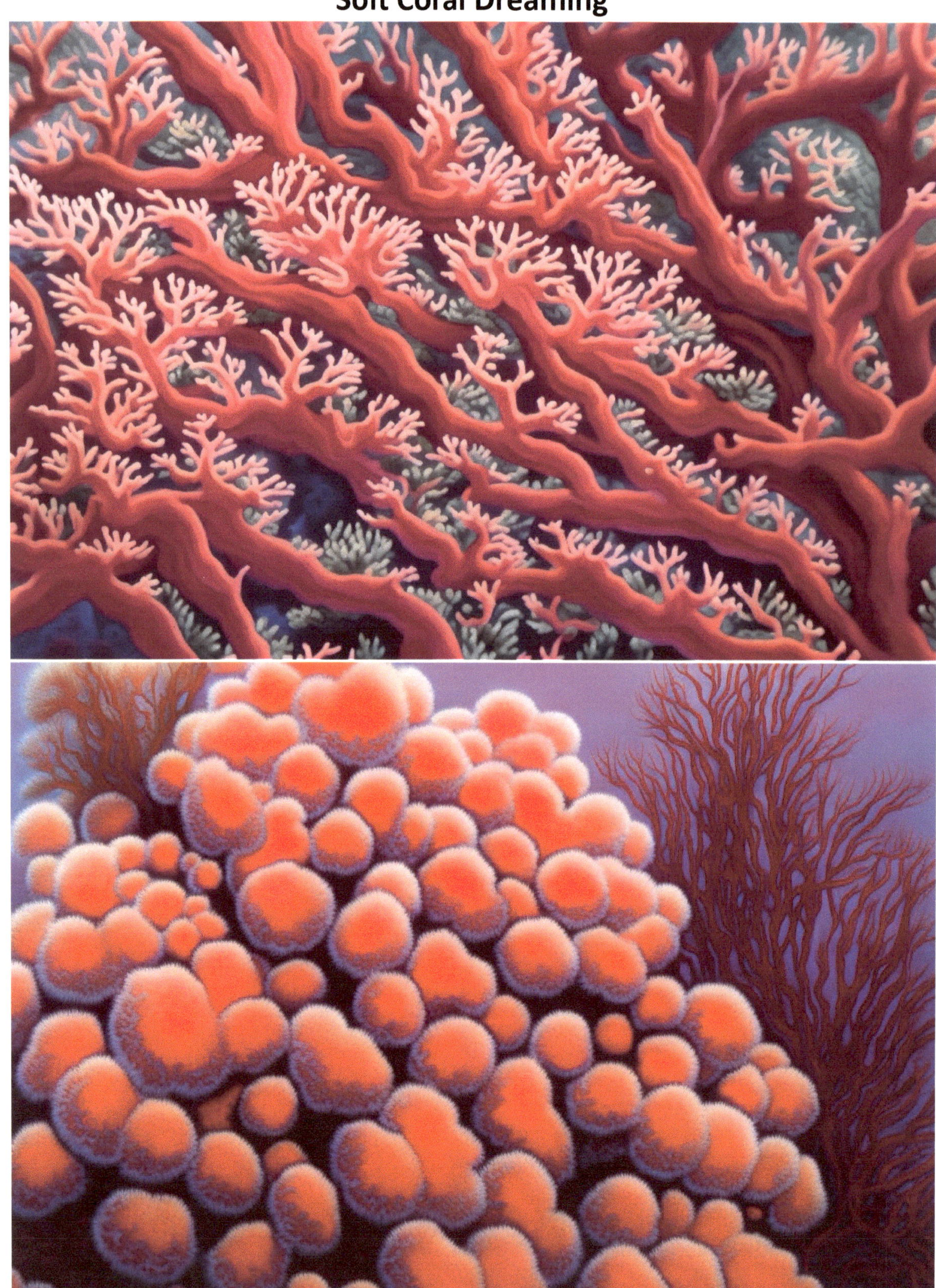

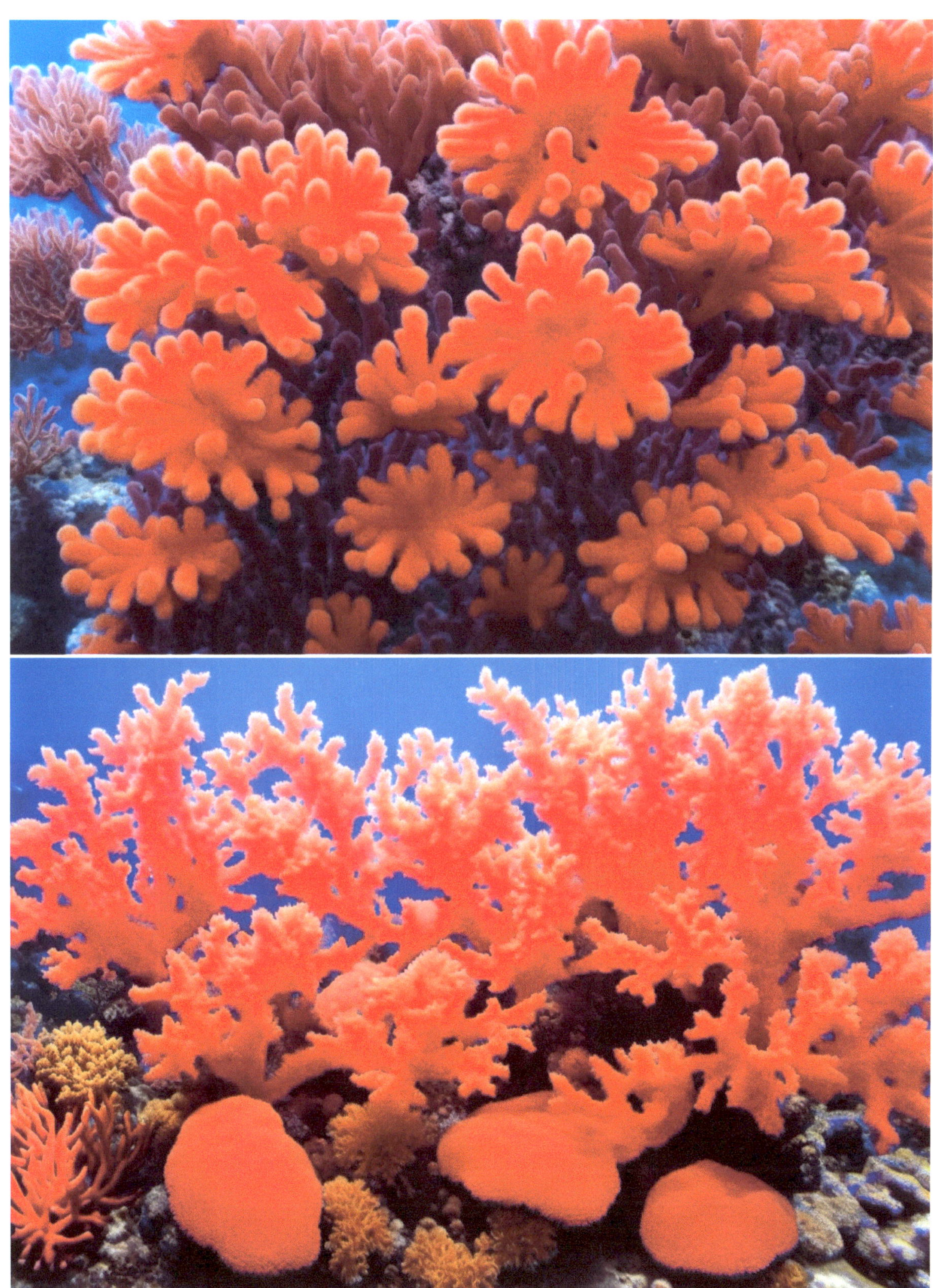

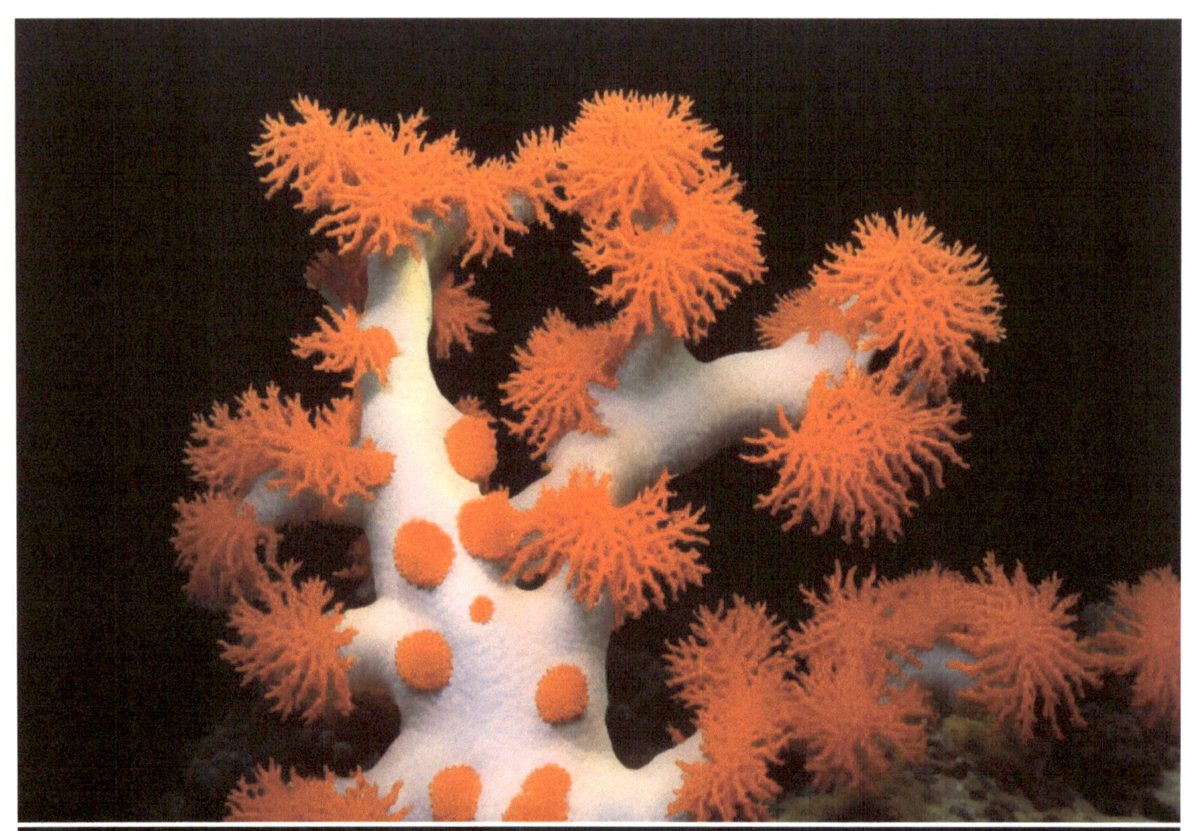

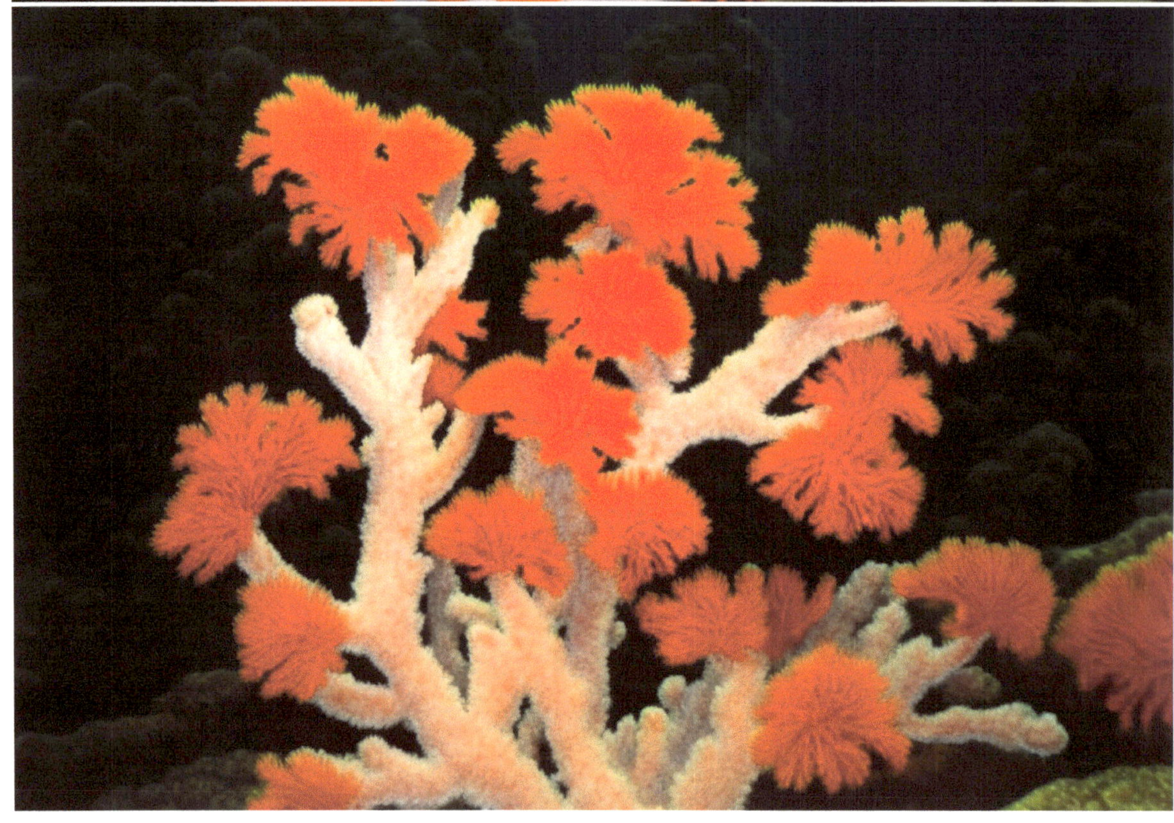

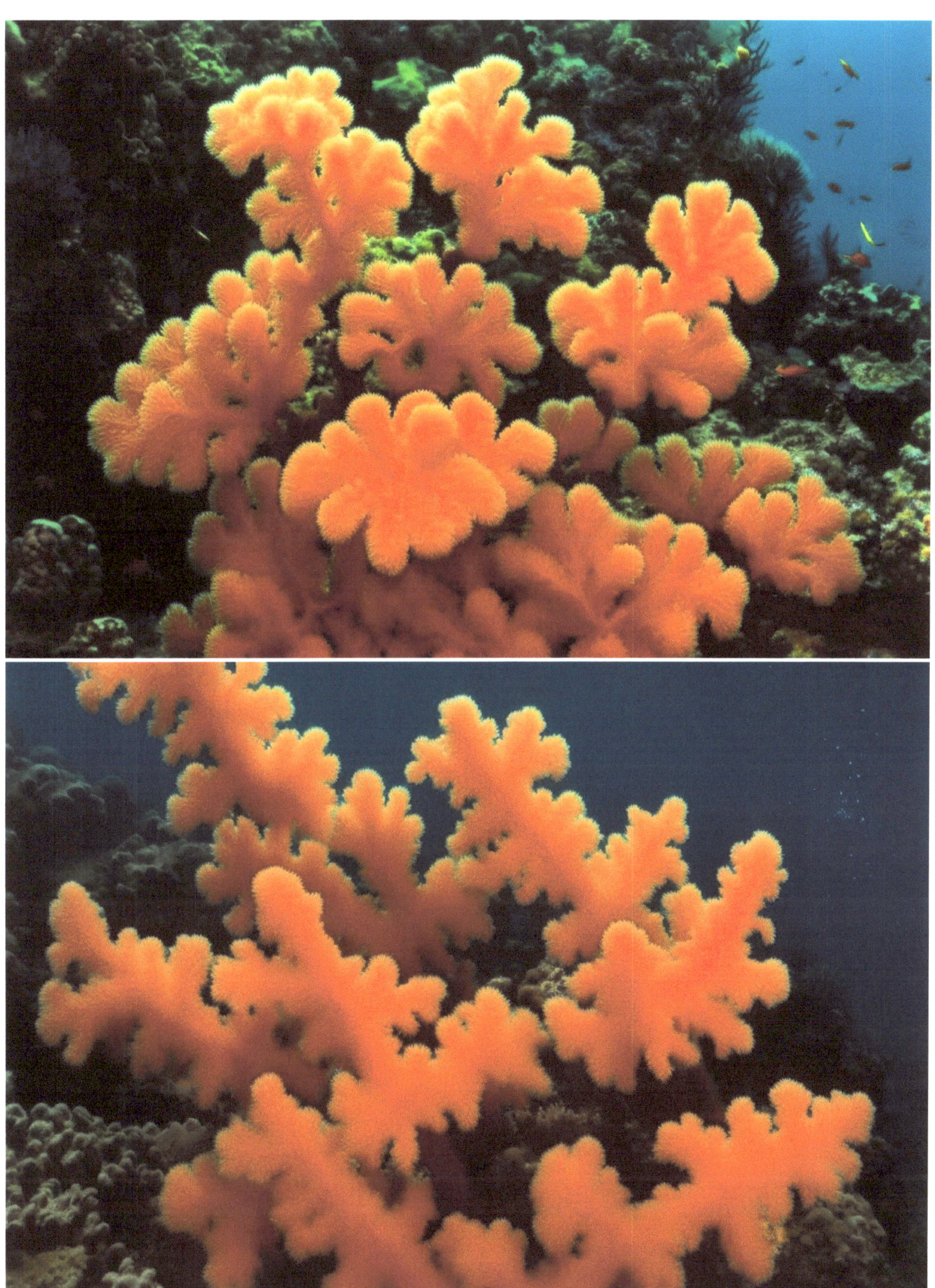

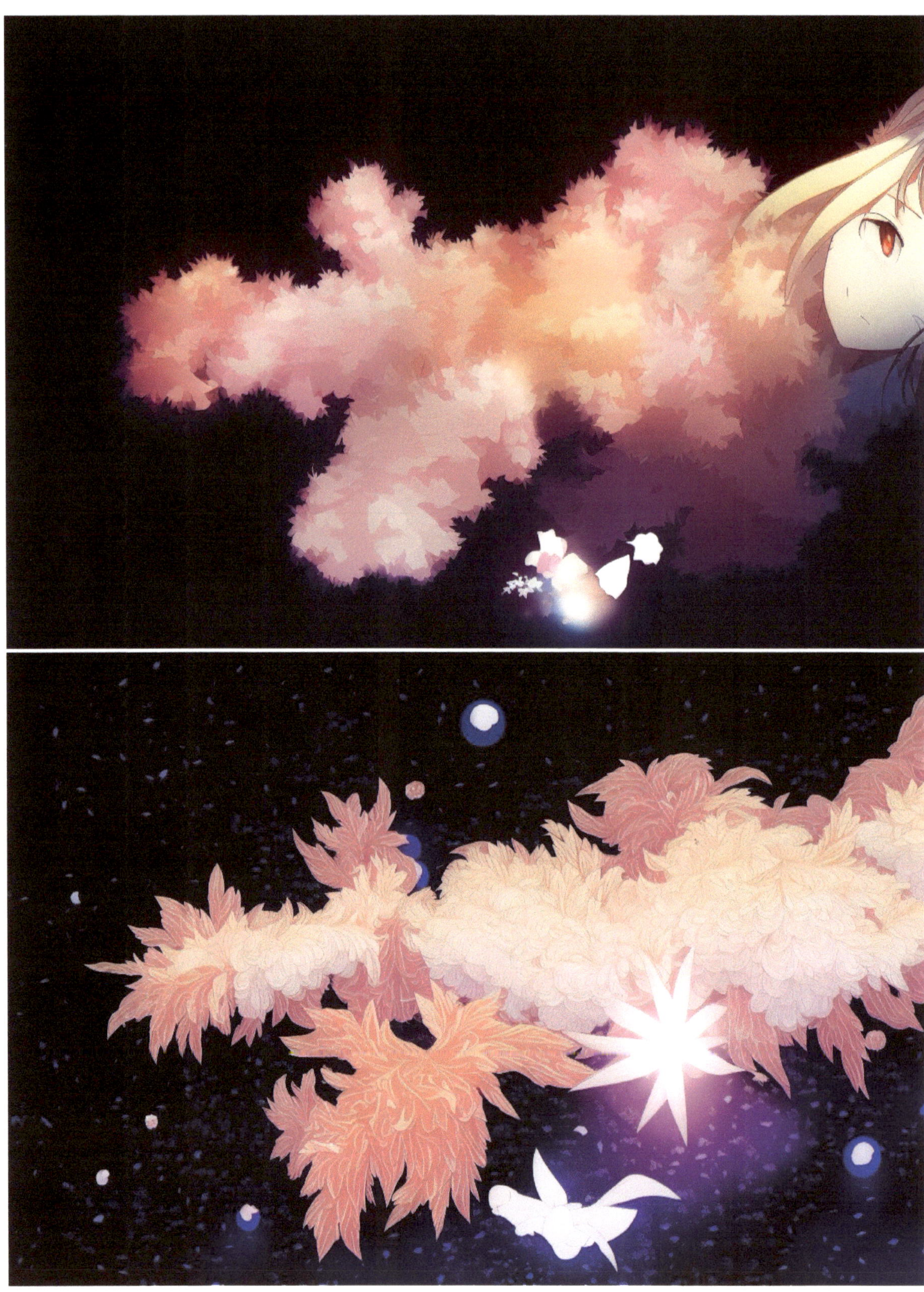

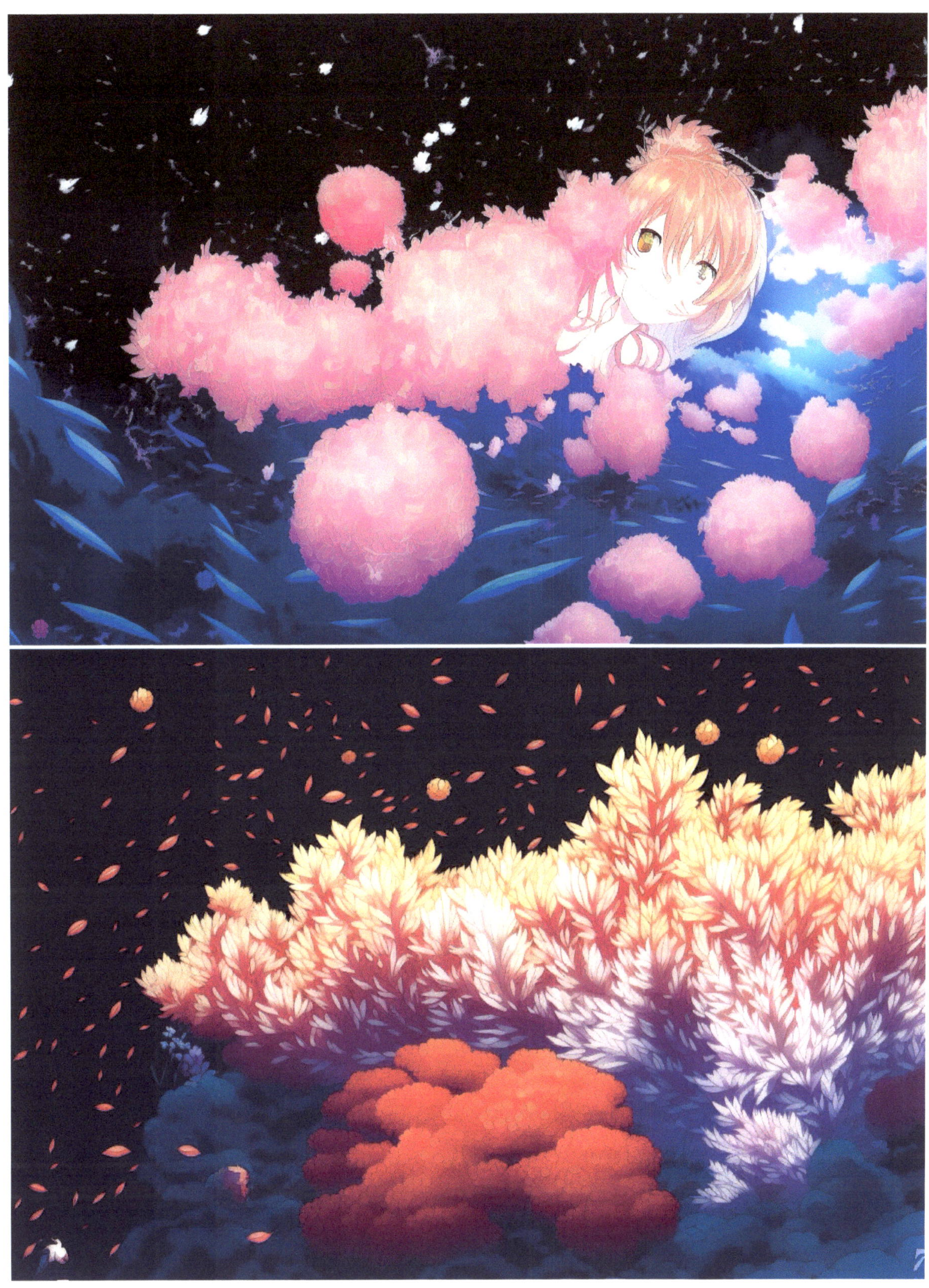

Starfish Dreaming

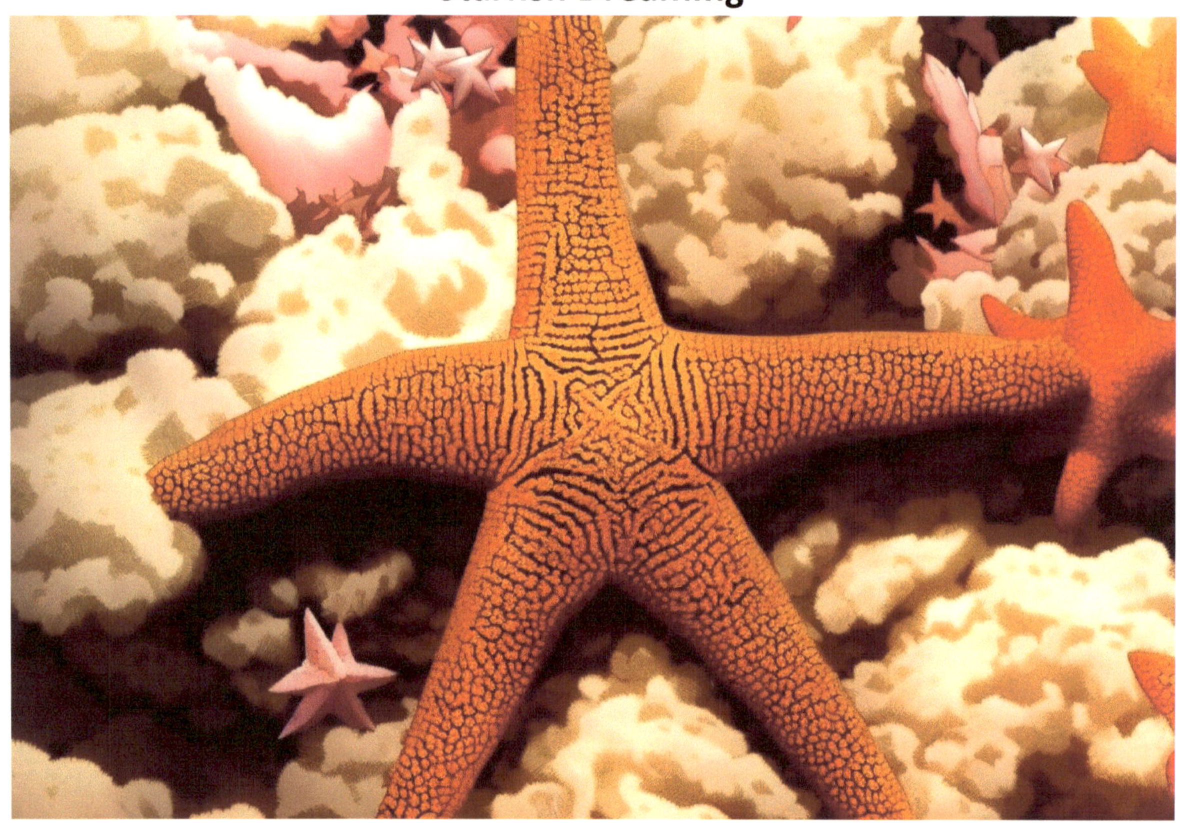

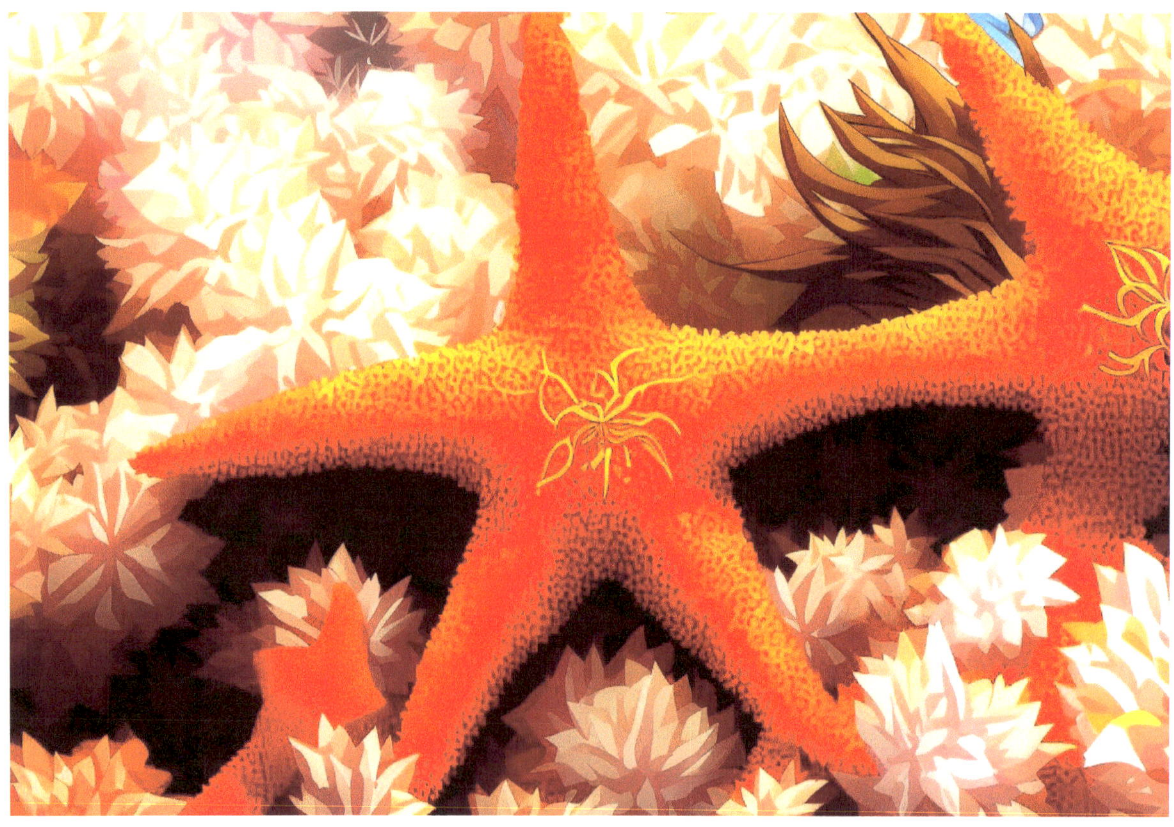

Hard Coral Dreaming

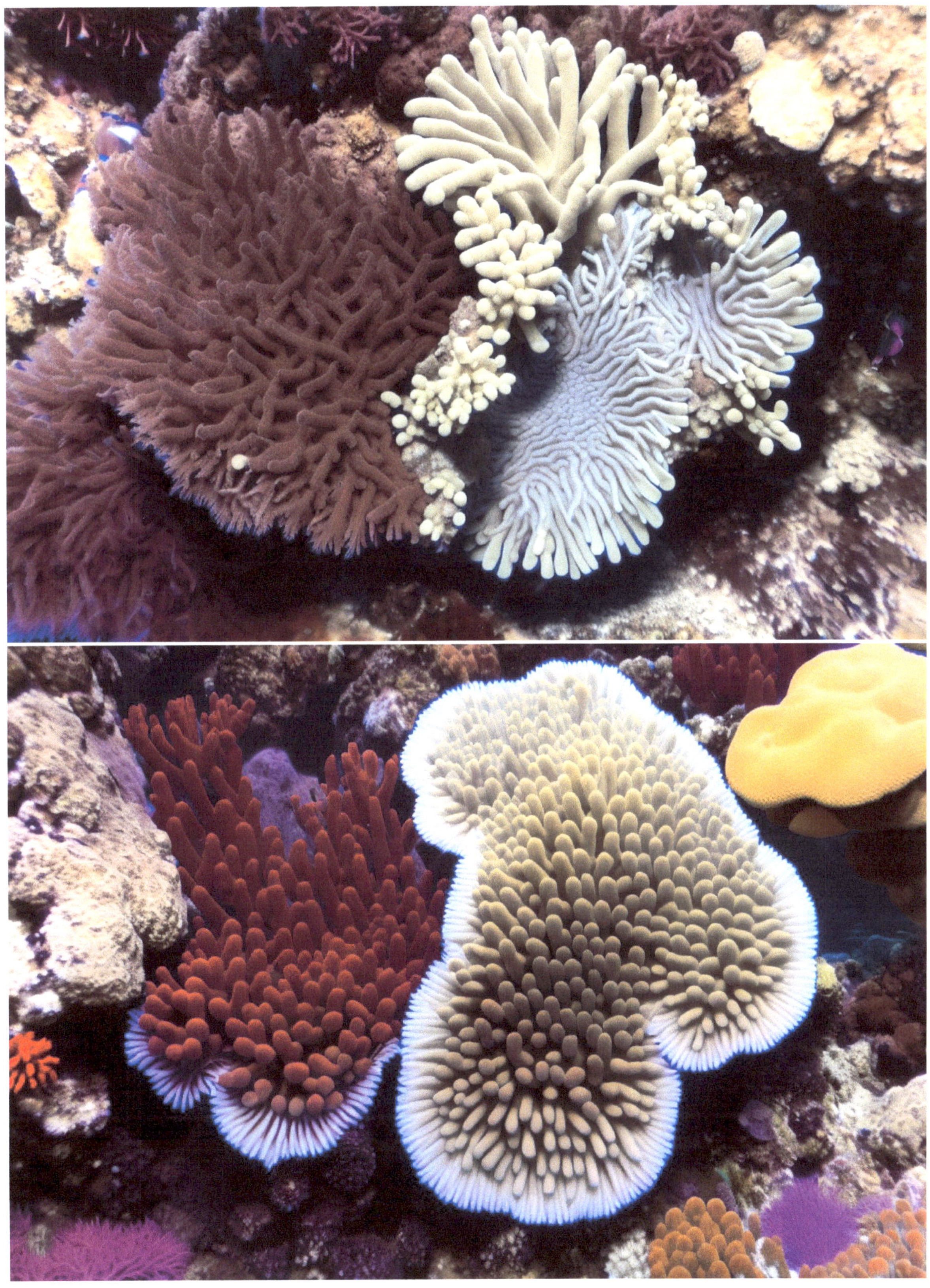

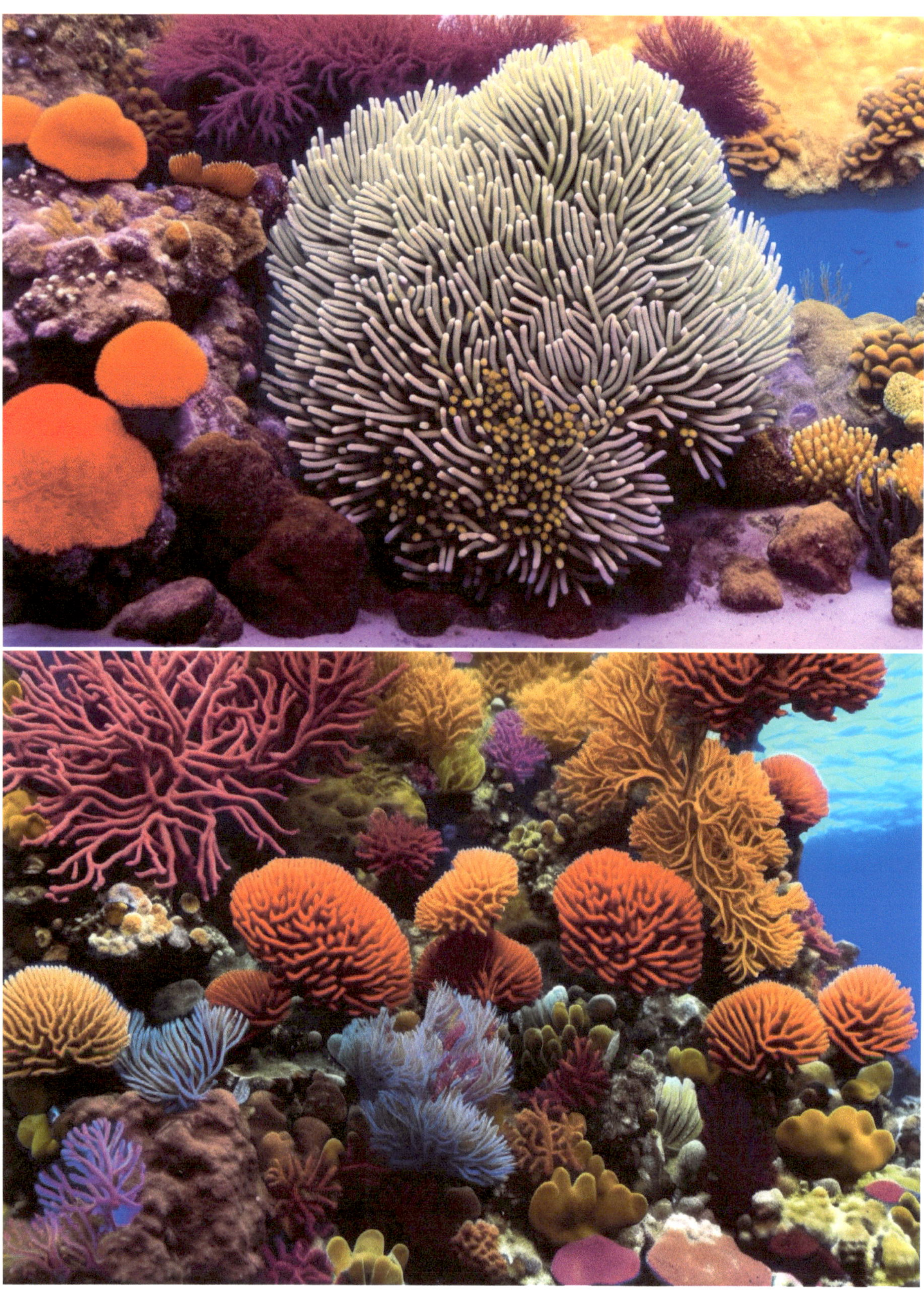

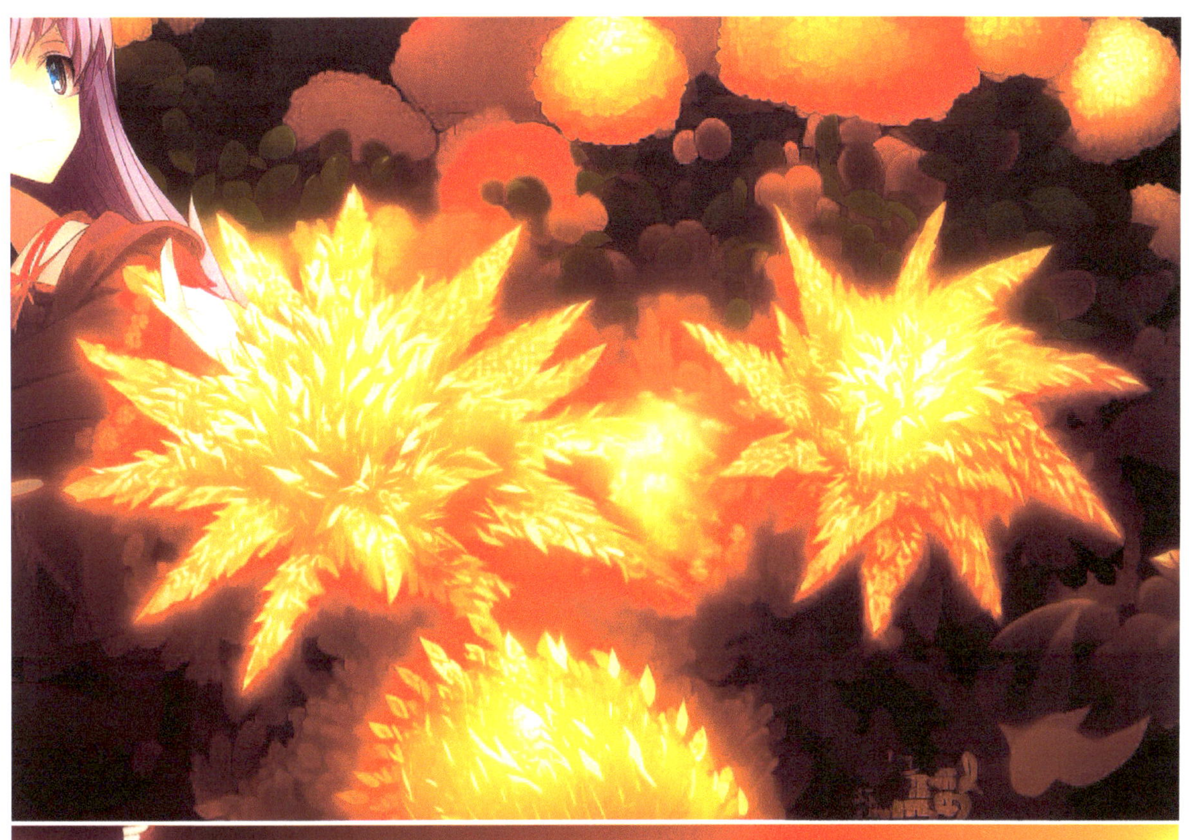

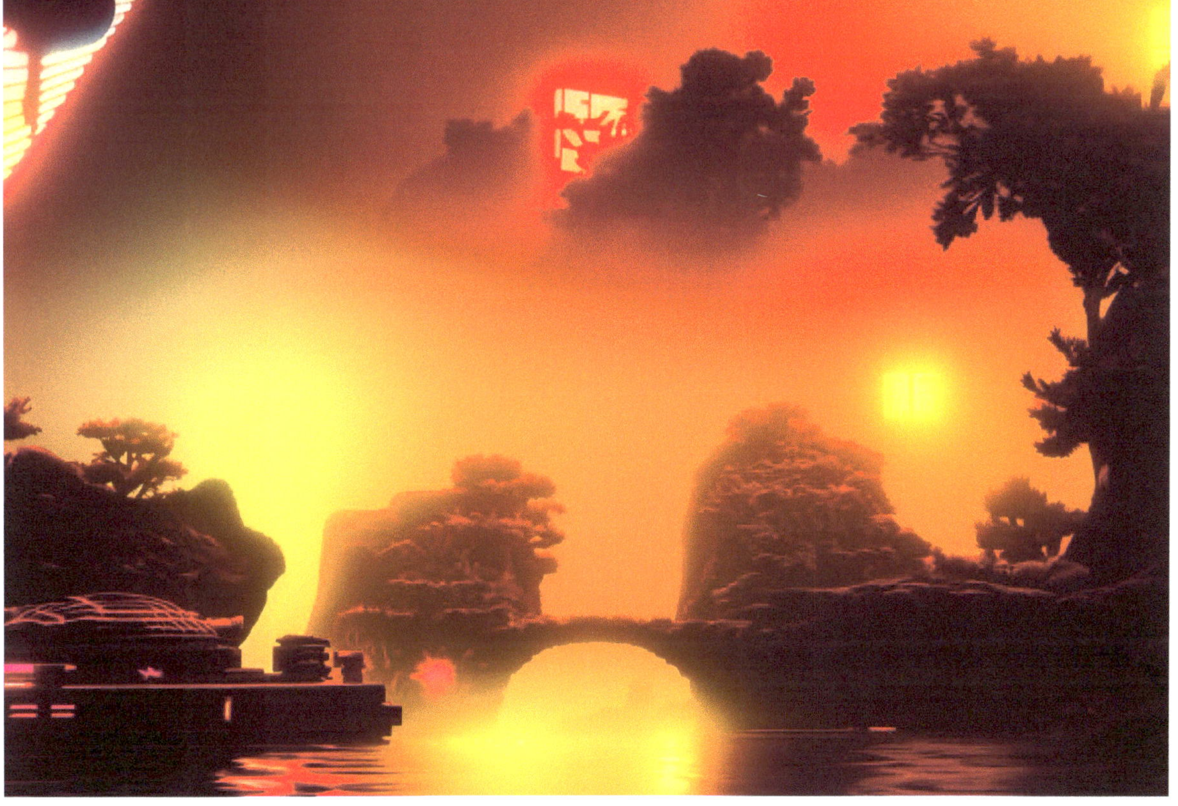

www.ingramcontent.com/pod-product-compliance
Ingram Content Group UK Ltd.
Pitfield, Milton Keynes, MK11 3LW, UK
UKHW060121300726
14090UKWH00002B/292

* 9 7 8 0 6 4 5 7 9 6 1 1 7 *